# The Meal of the Kingdom

*A Fresh Perspective on the Mysterious Power of the Lord's Supper*

By Ruben Torres

dragon
*tree*books

1620 SW 5th Avenue

Pompano Beach, Florida 33060

(954)788-4775

editors@editingforauthors.com

dragontreebooks.com

# Contents

# Introduction

When I think back on the initial conception of this book, I have to admit that my train of thought got started when I watched the movie *The Passion of the Christ*. As you may recall, that film displayed the suffering of Christ in a very gruesome and vivid way. The spectacle of Jesus' torture was so prominent that many criticized the film as being too graphic and cruel, and the public generally perceived that the production was full of senseless violence. In many ways, that's exactly what the cross was: pure cruelty, gore, and horror for no justifiable reason. If that isn't clearly communicated, one may never truly grasp the full significance and depth of Jesus' passion in death. What caught my attention when I saw the film was the way in which the director, Mel Gibson, portrayed the cross as an event that must be understood in the context of the Passover meal. The film jumped back and forth from the agony, pain, and suffering of Jesus to His life, His message, and His last moments with His disciples at the Last Supper. In other words, the movie was basically interpreting the cross in light of the sacrament of communion, and illuminating the power of communion in the context of the cross. That realization was like lightning flashing into my spirit. The message was always all about the cross, lived around the fellowship table of the Lord!

This was undeniable, and I had to ask myself in embarrassment if anything we are doing today as Christians had anything to do with the truth as it was presented in this motion picture. The honest answer was no, and as uncomfortable as it was to accept, I had to admit that very little of what today is celebrated in Christianity revolves around the vision of the broken body and the new covenant blood celebrated in the Lord's Supper. That is a significant observation, because in many ways to misunderstand the celebration and understanding of the Eucharist is to grievously wrong the entire Christian enterprise.

There are three fascinating facts that I discovered about communion that compelled me to see the importance of writing on this subject. Once you see these facts with me, I hope you'll realize how strange it is that these truths have been neglected, overlooked, and minimized within our contemporary Christian culture. Here is fact number one: from the earliest time of the church's history, the Lord's Supper has always been at the center of the true Christian faith, the pillar of its worship and the distinctive fruit of its particular devotion. Number two, not only did everything seem to revolve around the doctrine of the Lord's table from the very beginning, but the sacrament of partaking of the Lord's body was frequently celebrated in a reverential and practical manner within the first congregations of believers.[1] Lastly, number three, there is good evidence to conclude that the communities of believers that partook of holy communion strongly believed in the spiritual benefits and mystical experience of this ritual as having great significance for their faith because of its divine influence over their lives.[2] These three things cannot be easily ignored as trivial or peripheral to the faith of individuals; if taken seriously, their implications and consequences are huge for the general authenticity of our common

---

[1] Acts 2:42, 46-47. For those who reduced these activities to simply the practice of regular meals, the list of things described in these passages all seemed to be essential aspects of the church's spiritual devotion. At the very least, a sacramental allusion is in view, as affirmed regularly throughout the common testimony found in both books of Acts and Luke. (Luke 9:16, Luke 24:35, Luke 24:30, Acts 20:11, Acts 20:7, Acts 27:35). The three major branches of orthodox Christianity, which claim to historically be the most primitive, seem to all highly emphasize the sacrament of the Lord's Supper, constantly partaking of the meal as their primary act of worship in liturgical fashion.

[2] *A Dictionary of Early Christian Beliefs*, David W. Bercot, pgs. 251-259, 1998. Many church fathers throughout history attribute divine properties to the elements of the Lord's table (1 Corinthians 6:16-17, 1 Corinthians 10:21, 1 Corinthians 11:27-32). Something mystical is clearly attested to in these passages as occurring at the very moment of partaking of the bread and wine.

Christian worldview. Analyzing their repercussions critically and carefully, we can conclude that many of the activities we emphasize today as essential for our spiritual development have been, for the most part, removed from the central focus of the Lord's table. All this we can assert without having yet even discussed the meaning of the Eucharist, or what its value truly is. Nevertheless, we can still confront the reality that many people today go to church, worship, conference, preach, teach, and evangelize with no clear understanding of how any of these endeavors are supposed to be consummated within the sacramental life that is celebrated through holy communion.

This problem, at the very least, deserves to be addressed, and that is why I have ventured on this journey to fill this book with some of the many scriptural gems and pearls of insight that often seemed to be hidden in plain sight, out of our doctrinal consciousness. My main objective is to help readers view the sacrament of communion as the motivation behind all of our ecclesiastical ventures, and at the same time to stimulate believers to desire conformity to a more Biblical understanding of the meaning of belonging to a Christ-centered community.

# 1

# The Liturgical Nature and Priestly Order of the Lord's Supper

## Jesus, Minister of the Bread and Wine

This chapter contains some of the most impactful and fascinating insights that I have discovered throughout my research concerning the mystery of holy communion. Meditating on several Old Testament ideas mentioned throughout the Gospels[3] changed the way that I

---

[3] Namely temple ordinances, priesthood, worship, and sacrifices. Throughout the Gospel narratives, there is a connection between Jesus' life, his actions, and the meaning of the Old Testament protocols exercised in the temple. John 1:14 clearly alludes to Jesus as the tabernacling presence of God. Jesus dying in Passover as the Lamb of God is an easy allusion to how that feast of Israel was being consummated in his person (Luke 22:15-16, 1 Corinthians 5:7). Jesus' practice of forgiveness of sins was believed to be exclusively managed within the temple rituals and its priesthood (Matthew 12:8). Jesus' disciples don't observe the sabbath; in this setting, Jesus states that someone greater than the temple is with them. The implications are that God Himself, in a new redefined temple with a new order of principles and ministry, is at work (Matthew 22:51). At the moment of death, the temple veil was torn, connecting the events of the cross with the activity and spiritual reality that was encapsulated within the most holy place (Matthew 26:65). The high priest tore his clothes (Exodus 28:31-32, Leviticus 10:6, Leviticus 21:10), perhaps a subtle allusion to the transition of ministry taking place at that very moment, away from the Levitical priesthood and towards the new order of Melquizedek. Jesus himself quotes at that instance Psalm 110 and Daniel 7, implying the correct interpretation of the events that are about to transpire on the cross. Jesus was receiving power and authority, and being established as a new priest forever in the order of Melquizedek.

understood the rituals behind the Lord's Supper. Think along with me; according to the New Testament, who administers the elements of the body and blood of Jesus in the events leading up to the cross and the Last Supper? It is Jesus, as the high priest of our faith[4]. How should we understand Jesus as high priest in regards to the elements of bread and wine that he is blessing and instructing his followers to commemorate in remembrance of Him? Answer: Jesus apparently sees the participation at his table as an act of worship, an offering in the liturgical tradition of priestly sacrifices[5]. Amazing, right? Not only that, but something else also happened at the moment of the institution of the sacrament of holy communion. Jesus seemed to be establishing his disciples in a new, reimagined order of service to God. In other words, the old covenant was giving way to the new one; the old temple was being redefined and reconstituted by a new house for God in the body of the Messiah[6]. The traditional Levitical order of priesthood was being superseded by a more excellent and effective ministry, that of the Lord Himself and His representatives.

Jesus lived within the context of the world of Judaism; the paradigm through which he viewed His own identity, deeds, and words was the social structure and cultural background of Israel's history[7]. The vocation of the chosen people of God—the administration of the temple

---

[4] Hebrews 7:26, Hebrews 9:12-14, Hebrews 4:14, Hebrews 9:24, Hebrews 10:12.

[5] In Matthew 26:26, Jesus' blessing of the cup implies a divine element being conferred and administered in the participation of the wine, and 1 Corinthians 10:16 apparently confirms such interpretation. Matthew 26:28 clearly identifies the cup as the equivalent of a priestly offering, carrying the redemptive power of the remission of sins (Leviticus 24:5-9, Numbers 28:7, Exodus 24:9-11, Exodus 25:23-24, 29-30). The covenant was remembered with an offering meal of bread and wine exclusively delegated to the priest in the holy place (table of the presence); now there is a parallel model in the new covenant celebrated in the Last Supper, and it is described like a new table of show bread, "a memorial of the covenant." It is also to be remembered by a new breed of priests in the Lord's disciples.

[6] John 2:19, John 14:1-6. In the context of the whole gospel of John, a good argument can be made that Jesus Himself is the house of the Father, and the place he is preparing by His spirit is the dwelling of His presence in us, like that of the Father in Him.

[7] *The New Testament and the People of God*, NT Wright, chapter 16, page 468, 1992.

and the glory that was supposed to reside within it—was always in His mind. I have come to realize that only within that Biblical setting can we truly comprehend the frame of mind of Jesus and the priestly theology of the New Testament. The bread and wine, the body and blood, the cross and fellowship at the Lord's table are all interpreted in scripture to be the consummation and fulfillment of the Old Testament prophecies that predicted the marriage between Heaven and Earth in the eternal union of God and His people[8]. That's what happened at the cross, and that's what is celebrated and commemorated at the Lord's Supper. Just like in the temple of old, but now with a new mediator in the form of a human and divine priest, we are able to achieve a union with God that is reminiscent of the unity that exists within God Himself[9]. A powerful picture emerges when we accept the remembrance of Jesus' sacrifice as an act of worship that our High Priest ordained for us to enjoy alongside Him. We, as the Israel of God, the new temple of the Holy Spirit, ministers of the new covenant, reflectors of God's image, a kingdom of priests unto our God, are supposed to offer sacrifices to the Lord that present evidence of our true Christian worship. What are we supposed to offer up in this new temple? What is our distinctive new covenant worship? It is the re-enactment and actualization of the life, presence, and sacrifice of Jesus in a sacramental manner.

What we are discussing is that there should be some understanding of a liturgical and ritualistic dimension behind all of the church's structures and devotions. Everything we do within our faith is supposed to reflect the meaning of Jesus' vision of communion and his example of a sacrificial lifestyle. Our temple is not without an offering, and our assembly is not without the ministry of some specific spiritual ordinances. Bread and wine are more than elements in a particular community meal that we celebrate once a month. These elements are supposed to serve as a reminder of the meaning of the cross, the significance

---

[8] Isaiah 54:5-8, 10, Hosea 2:15-20, Jeremiah 2:1-2, Ezekiel 16:8, Jeremiah 31:31-34, Jeremiah 33:10-11, 14-17. The new covenant is connected in scripture to the motif of a spiritual marriage. Jesus is seen in the New Testament as the bridegroom (Mark 2:19-20, Revelation 19:7, Matthew 25:1-13, John 3:28-30).

[9] John 17:22-24, Hebrews 2:17-18, Hebrews 7:24-28.

of Christ's glorification in new creation, and the church's reason for existence. Perhaps the problem has been that, because Jesus is generally understood to undermine and relativize the Old Testament's dogmas and restrictions, people conclude that Christianity should avoid any element of spiritual order in liturgical practices. Nothing can be further from the truth. Jesus Himself said: "Do not think that I have come to abolish the Law or the Prophets; I have not come to abolish them but to fulfill them" (Matthew 5:17).

That is the same as saying: Don't think that I have come to remove and do away with all the things that you hold most precious and important; I am literally here to make those dreams a reality, so you can truly live to enjoy them.

If anything, if we have in Jesus the true substance of what the old covenant only alluded to symbolically, then our reverential approach to God should be even higher in awareness and focus than all the examples of consecration seen in the former temple and its priesthood[10]. Let's pause and get practical for a moment. Are we saying that we should celebrate and partake more often of the bread and wine of Jesus in our services in order to become truly orthodox Christians? Are we implying that without regular communion services, we are not engaging in authentic Biblical worship? Not necessarily. I think what we are trying to convey is that we should see ourselves and all of our expressions of faith as an extension and representation of the Lord Himself and His heavenly ministry, which is emblemized at the Lord's Supper. We should reconsider with a fresh perspective all the ways in which our words, deeds, and service can be grounded and centered around the revelation of holy communion. That way, we would not only desire to partake more often of the meal of the kingdom[11], but we would also seek ways to reconcile our ministerial efforts with the aim of promoting the union with God that is promised to be manifested at the Lord's loving feast[12].

---

[10] Hebrews 10:29, Hebrews 8:1-3, 6, Hebrews 9:11-12, 24-26.

[11] Luke 22:18.

[12] Jude 1:12; the agape. Early Christians celebrated a community meal reminiscent of the Eucharist as part of their church gatherings.

## *The Roots of Sacrifice and Ritual Behind Holy Communion*

To begin diving into some of the topics of this chapter, let's ask ourselves some specific questions. Since the Lord's Supper is better understood scripturally as the Earthly illustration of the eternal sacrifice of our heavenly priest[13], how are we to celebrate and unite ourselves with this offering in a Biblical manner? Also, to whom exactly is this offering being dedicated as we commemorate its remembrance? To answer these questions, perhaps we should take into account some of the principles found in the Old Testament scriptures in regards to the offerings, the temple, and the ministry of priests that were prepared unto the Lord. For example, in the story of Israel's calling[14], we see how the priesthood was consecrated to God, separated uniquely as His own possession[15]. Not only that, but also all of the priests' service was directed exclusively unto the Lord as holy acts of worship[16]. The furniture inside the tabernacle, including the ark, the altar of incense, the menorah, and the bread and wine in the table of propitiation were all anointed and dedicated to God as His distinctive property, used entirely for His own inhabiting delight[17]. This could easily be overlooked or ignored as an unimportant detail, but this idea of belonging to God for His glory and pleasure is continued in the New Testament, which describes our status and purpose before God[18]. Here is a revolutionary thought that

---

[13] 1 Corinthians 10:18, Hebrews 13:10-13. Union with Jesus' sacrifice celebrated in communion is compared to the old covenant altar. Both scriptures are used as analogies for how unity with God was achieved through the sacrifices made on the altar, and now those sacrifices are consummated in Christ's ministry.

[14] Exodus 19:5-6, Deuteronomy 4:20, Deuteronomy 7:6, Deuteronomy 10:15, Deuteronomy 14:2, Deuteronomy 26:18-19, Psalms 135:4. In the same manner, the New Testament speaks of the people of God who belong to Christ (Titus 2:14, 1 Peter 2:9).

[15] Deuteronomy 10:8, Numbers 8:20-21, Numbers 8:14-18, Numbers 18:20-24.

[16] Numbers 3:3, Numbers 4:4-15, Exodus 29:1-9, 21, 29.

[17] Exodus 29:43-45.

[18] Romans 15:16, 2 Corinthians 2:15, 2 Timothy 4:6, Philippians 2:17, Ephesians 1:12, 14, Romans 12:1, 1 Corinthians 6:20, Acts 20:28, Revelation 5:9, 1 Peter 1:18-21, Romans 14:7-8, Philippians 1:20. In 2 Corinthians 5:14-15, we are purchased as His possession for His glory, and ought to live as such.

we might fail to consider as relevant when we attempt to celebrate the Lord's Supper: Jesus, as our High Priest, was offering in the elements of communion not only Himself, but us[19] to be presented to our God as an offering of sacrifice and worship for His glory[20]. The table, like the entirety of Christian life, is supposed to be a giving over of ourselves in consecration to God[21]. Jesus' whole life and purpose could be characterized as a commitment of veneration in complete abandonment and surrender to God's will[22]. In like manner, the invitation to the Lord's table is an appeal for us to join Him in His sacrifice, reflecting and assimilating His posture, disposition, and commitment of adulation in passion for God[23]. We can deduce that when approaching the bread and wine, the body and blood of Jesus, our mindset should be one of rendition, following the example of the Lord with humility by giving ourselves completely to God in seeking union with Christ. This understanding of being one with Christ's offering of love changes our perspective, making us more yielded and reverent when interacting with the elements of communion. This is not supposed to be a mechanical exercise of mysticism to calm our conscience, performed out of spiritual indifference. Often, we wrongly approach the Lord's table as a kind of mysterious formula to get undeserved results or rewards for our religious convenience. Our union with the elements of communion goes beyond the obedience of following an antiquated command, because

---

[19] 1 Corinthians 10:17, 1 Corinthians 11:29; we are part of the body that needs to be discerned in the elements. In John 17:21-22, Jesus' prayer focuses on His glorification and His departure, desiring for the disciples to see His glory and join Him to enjoy through His ministry the unity He shares with the Father.

[20] Hebrews 9:14, Ephesians 5:2, Hebrews 13:15, 1 Peter 2:5, Ephesians 3:21, Hebrews 10:5-10, Hebrews 9:23-24, John 17:24, Colossians 1:22, Ephesians 5:27.

[21] Colossians 3:17, 1 Corinthians 10:31, Ephesians 5:20, Colossians 3:23, 1 Peter 4:11.

[22] John 12:23-24, 27, Mark 10:45, John 17:4, John 4:34, John 5:30, John 6: 38. Jesus lived to glorify God and do His will.

[23] Luke 9:23, Luke 14:27, Matthew 10:38, 39. The cross and the table are connected in meaning and symbolism; they are interchangeable as models for the Christian life (Galatians 2:20, Galatians 5:24, Galatians 6:14, 2 Corinthians 4:10, 11, Romans 6:6, 1 Peter 2:21, 24).

we are literally engaging with the divine nature of the son of God by faith, partaking of the essence of His supernatural worship.

Now let us continue our investigation of the Old Testament to illuminate the foundations behind the tradition of sacrificial offerings. One key story about the significance of sacrifice is found in Abraham's offering of Isaac. This tale encapsulates one of the greatest mysteries of the Bible, presenting a portrait of the revelation of worship found through offerings. Throughout the Genesis record, we find that the shedding of blood was first instituted by God Himself in the covering of animal skins that he provided for Adam[24]. Interestingly, when we reach the tale of the Akedah, Isaac asks his father about the burnt offering they are supposed to present to God, and Abraham answers an echo of the Genesis account by saying that God himself will provide the lamb[25]. That is to say: what was instituted from the beginning is happening again, because only God Himself can execute divine covering, confer supernatural exchange, and establish holy communion in worship[26]. The knowledge of the power of burnt offerings was apparently present in Abraham's heart and mind when he prepared for his journey to bind Isaac in the altar.[27]

What exactly is this knowledge that Abraham possessed about burnt offerings? And what can this insight tell us about the practice and implementation of the Lord's Supper? We see in scripture how the

---

[24] Genesis 3:21.

[25] Genesis 22:8. It was prefigured from the beginning that the most excellent sacrifice is that of the blood of the mysterious lamb that God Himself provides for the divine covering, remission, and restitution of a relationship with Himself.

[26] The instruction and ordinance of burnt offerings was not a secret in the Genesis narrative. Cain and Abel were judged on the merits of the content, execution, and intentions behind their offerings. The implication is that they had knowledge of the correct and incorrect ways of presenting themselves before God.

[27] Genesis 15:9. All the species of animals that were commanded to be offered in the tabernacle of Moses are represented in Abraham's covenant offering. All five types of offerings that were instructed to be observed in this tabernacle also seemed to be illustrated throughout Abraham's life. Meal offering: Genesis 14:18-19. Peace offering: Genesis 18:6-8. Burn offering: Genesis 22:2. Guilt and sin offerings were encapsulated in Genesis 15:9, which represents the entirety of the sacrificial system.

rites and observances of veneration through offerings did not originate with the tabernacle of Moses. These customs of approaching the divine through the formality of immolation go all the way back to the beginning of time in the Garden. Seemingly, it was from those traditions that Abraham was finding inspiration to properly intertwine himself with the supernatural presence of God. From the very dawn of creation, it was God Himself who taught the principle of offering up a transaction of exchange from the life force of the blood to provide a covering[28]. Every other repetition of this practice was also an attempt to emulate and follow the pattern of that premier offering, by having the presence of God inhabit and consummate the sacrifices. When Abraham stated the revelation that God will provide, he attested to the insight of true worship that could only be validated by God Himself. The father of faith was joining the experience that was concealed deep within the heart of God, by surrendering the most precious thing he had in his life, handing over the closest and dearest offering anyone could give: the affection of love found in his only Son. Notice how Scripture subtly alludes to this hidden truth when it affirms:

> *"Since he did not spare even his own Son, but gave him up for us all, won't he also give us everything else? Who dares accuse us whom God has chosen for his own? No one—for God himself has given us right standing with himself. Who then will condemn us? No one—for Christ Jesus died for us and was raised to life for us, and he is sitting in the place of honor at God's right hand, pleading for us" (Romans 8:32-34 NLT).*

Do you catch the pattern? God Himself provided for Adam, for Abraham, and for the rest of humanity in the giving of the Son, because only He can effectuate the true divine transaction of right standing with Him in the divine revelation of worship. Abraham was embracing the mystery of divine communion that exists within God's nature by not only representing, but assimilating the love of the Father for

---

[28] Leviticus 17:11.

the Son, when he gave Isaac over. Like Abraham, when we approach the Lord's table, we are encouraged to join the mystery of worship that resides inside the heart of God, giving our all for Him in the same way He gave His best for us.

Now with this foundation in mind, let us attempt to take inventory of some particular principles of sacrifice learned through the Genesis account that reach a climax in the tale of Abraham and Isaac. If Jesus' covenant meal is truly to be regarded within the Old Testament context as a sacrificial offering, we would do well to examine the depth of meaning behind these ordinances and practices from their very inception.

*1. Altars were a place of confrontation.* They gave a dose of sobriety, allowing people to face reality and grounding life into new spiritual consciousness[29]. Idols are removed, inner conflicts are exposed, human sensibility is recovered. The tone of the Genesis narrative is a serious summoning of hearts into introspection before God, frequently calling humanity to account for their actions and attitudes[30]. In the book of beginnings, the altar becomes the avoided place where man is vulnerable to the divine presence of God, dealing with life and its consequences as unavoidable interactions with God. The failure of humanity to take ownership and responsibility for its degenerate inclinations and susceptibilities was apparently supposed to be addressed in sacrifice[31]. In Abraham's case, he had to look deep within himself to scrutinize his convictions and dispositions. Was God first in his life? Above all else, including his promises? This motif of confrontation is not exclusive to the Old Testament patriarch; it is also echoed in the altar of communion in the fellowship table of the Lord. When we partake of the

---

[29] Genesis 3:21-22, Genesis 4:6-7. The covering of Adam was a confrontation with his nakedness, while the encounter of Cain with God was a confrontation with His state of mind and heart after his offering.

[30] Genesis 6:5.

[31] Genesis 3:8-12, 13. Adam was hiding, unable to repent or show remorse for his actions, so God dealt with the state of his heart with new coverings. In Genesis 4:6, 9-10, we find the same scenario: the hidden iniquity, left unaddressed, hardened the heart, presumably because of the failure to engage correctly in the divine transaction of sacrifice.

breaking of bread, it is said that we ought to discern the body. That is why you should examine yourself before eating the bread and drinking the cup. "But if we would examine ourselves, we would not be judged by God in this way" (1 Corinthians 11:28, 31 NLT).

Just like how the death of an animal was supposed to move the penitent to empathy for the creature that was offered, realizing that its death had to take place and be managed correctly in order to realign the life of the worshiper back to God, the participants at the table of communion are meant to reflect on the ultimate offering that God Himself provided for humanity, confronting every hidden issue that might hinder our relationship with Him.

*2. Altars were a place of exchange, where faith, hope, and love were tested in a divine transaction that confirms how the life of the worshiper relies totally on God for the promises of His future.* Death for life, sin for propitiation, shame for covering, the temporal for the eternal, the present for the future. There is an element of expectation in the altar of sacrifice, looking forward to the moment when the problems of death, sin, and decay will be fully addressed and resolved by God. As the burnt offering was consummated by fire, it was literally destroyed; in a sense, this represented the fall of all things in creation. Then, later, the offering was transformed into a different state, symbolized by the smoke that was received by God in a transcendent aroma. It is as if through the offering, the original intention of creation and the hidden meaning of all existence was returning back to God. He receives the essence of it all, because He is the only one who can one day restore it again to fulfill its original destiny.

Abraham knew he would burn and consume his son on the altar of sacrifice, yet he told the servants that they would both return after worship. That could only mean he had faith in a supernatural resurrection of his son Isaac[32]. In the Akedah, Abraham states: "It is God who will bring into completion all of His promises in the future, and for that

---

[32] Hebrews 10:11. Abraham believed, and was looking for new creation (Genesis 22:5, Hebrews 11:17-19).

complete fulfillment to take place in His glorious purpose a new world will be required. One where death, sin, and decay will no longer corrupt the good order of creation." In other words, if apprehending the future meant dying in the present, Abraham was willing to make the transaction in a supernatural exchange, offering his natural son for the resurrected one. That means for us today that the Earth, with all of its beauty and splendor, means nothing without a proper connection and relationship with its creator. In the altar of offerings, the transaction is made, dying in the natural state of things in anticipation of God's ultimate eternal future. Again we see a parallel, in the connection with our New Testament altar of worship in the sacrament of holy communion.

In the Lord's Supper, we are literally feasting on new creation; we are interacting with God's future, and preparing ourselves in anticipation of His royal appearance. "For every time you eat this bread and drink this cup, you are announcing the Lord's death until he comes again" (1 Corinthians 11:26 NLT).

We are being faithful witnesses and stewards of the elements of the resurrected life of the Messiah, until all the full glory and power of His new creation are manifested in His return.

*3. Altars were the place of covenant, where the terms and conditions of our relationship with God were stipulated by promises*[33]. Approaching the divine involved protocols, ordinances, and formalities that were established by the creator himself. All these precepts and rituals were structures within the format of a consensus that involved commitments and conditions. Approaching God by offerings was a way of actively pursuing a relationship with the creator. There isn't any room for any other gods in the worship of YHWH; this altar is exclusive and absolute, and

---

[33] Genesis 3:22-24. After the clothing of the skin, the relationship between man and God is said to be rearranged with new stipulations and promises (Genesis 4:3-5). Cain and Abel were celebrating their status through offerings before God, based on the covenantal agreements established in the garden (Genesis 8:20-22). The sacrifice of Noah was the precursor of a covenant relationship that released God's promises over the Earth and over his life (Genesis 12:7, Genesis 13:14-18, Genesis 15:17-18). Covenant promises are found in relation to altars and sacrifices.

it involves a serious binding and joining with the deity. In a world full of chaos, uncertainty, fear, and danger, to have any form of guarantee that the connection with the creator is secure and reliable is a lovely commodity. How much more serious can a person be about their commitment to God than depriving themselves of something very special, unique, and valuable, relying completely on the trustworthiness of their God? Abraham was following God's instructions in his offering of Isaac, but he also understood there were already arrangements involved in his worship. If Abraham was so passionate about his fidelity to God, he could rest in certainty that his maker was also going to remain faithful to all his promises. God made commitments to Abraham through the altar of sacrifice, and in each encounter of divine communion, his faith was growing and being strengthened to trust solely in the Lord's provision. Again, that is why the father of faith declared confidently to Isaac that the Lord himself would provide the lamb. In the Lord's Supper, God Himself is also making provision for us in sacrifice, giving us guarantee that He is sanctioning our deliverance, restoration, and eternal union with Him by his own name. This is a beautiful aspect of joining in the table of communion, because we are resting in God's pledge of love for us and feasting in His promises.

*4. Altars are a place for gratitude in worship, where remembrance is done in expressions of love that celebrate and give back to God everything He has given to us.* Often it is hard to understand why sacrifice is the equivalent of worship in the Bible. But if one recognizes the symbolism behind the giving of a life back to the giver of life, it is easier to grasp the connection. Sacrifice acknowledges that no other being is worth the spending or the taking of a life other than God, because he is the giver and sustainer of it all. Worship in relation to immolation states there is no moral or rational justification for existence or meaning apart from the owner and source of all things, who reserves the right of taking and giving everything in creation. Since the creator has chosen to freely give, then we in gratitude choose to freely give back to Him in a reenactment of the love and power he exerts over all things. In the very moment of creation, there is a question that requires analysis: namely, what is going to be the relationship between God and everything else that exists? Since God is self-sustaining, He needs nothing outside of Himself, and everything else in creation owes its existence to Him, depending on Him for sustenance. Therefore, the natural response to Him should be one of complete surrender and passionate adulation.

Worship is a totally unique endeavor seeking to relate and approach the divine in the correct manner of gratitude, affirming His unshared category of incorruptible holiness and eternal sovereignty. The proper posture that reconciles God to His creation is done in worship when, by the illustration of sacrifice, the creature that embodies nature freely and willingly recognizes the maker of it all, reflecting back to Him all His power, attributes, and characteristics hidden in creation. In approaching the creator, the ultimate act of humility is the total surrender of oneself, represented in the giving of something of value—in this case, a life, illustrating our lives in His presence. By yielding that which is precious with complete investment of the heart and soul, we are joining nature and all of creation in the submission of returning back to our source. We become like that creature in the altar, having no purpose outside of the pleasure of the one who made all things for His glory; we surrender in the offering with the sacrifice, not living any longer for ourselves but for Him, who gave us everything in life. This principle illuminates Abraham's actions; as he climbed Mount Moriah, he saw his submission to God as an act of worship. He was prostrating himself before the maker, returning all things back to the source, finding delight, gratitude, and purpose in his alignment to God, and discovering how his father and son relationship mirrored something deeper than the temporal enjoyment of his earthly existence.

When we approach the Lord's table, we are celebrating the event at which the creator inhabited His creation and, as our representative and substitute, reconciled all things back unto Himself. The high priest of our faith modeled for us the response of gratitude and thanksgiving that is reminiscent of the attitude and disposition of true worship, in the consecration of the elements. The giver of all things and the sustainer of all existence gave Himself as nourishment so that we may join him in remembrance of His love, through the sacrament that embodies the perfect alignment back with our source.

## *The Power and Significance of Ceremonial Rituals*

We have seen that before there was a temple, a priesthood, and the formal ordinances for worship in Israel, there was already the ritual of sacrifice. These spiritual roots of protocol serve as the foundation of understanding to grasp the intentions and objectives of the worshipers as they were approaching God in the Old Testament. Jesus' Last Supper celebration was literally a Passover meal, which itself commemorated the sacrifice of a consecrated lamb that was instituted by God to deliver Israel from death and redeem the people of God out of Egypt. That elaborated and sacred enactment, which was kept solemnly throughout the nation, looked back at the redemptive power of sacrifice, and it also looked forward, serving as an instructive narrative for our understanding and treatment of the Lord's table. Apparently, in Scripture God always delivers through sacrifice, and that divine redemptive action is perpetually preserved and commemorated in a ritualistic manner. From the selection of the animal to the method by which the animal is presented, bound, and slain upon the altar, there is an allusion to the language of symbolism, invoking meaning, order, and spiritual supervision behind the activity of immolation. At the communion celebration, Jesus, our high priest, established a new language by which we ought to approach the divine in our spiritual devotion. He exemplifies in His symbolic actions with the elements of bread and wine the way to understand his death, and the way to administrate His sacrifice in relationship towards God and others. In the day that the deliverance of Israel was formally commemorated, Jesus gave His disciples the true meaning of God's ultimate redemption, to forever be remembered in His presence with new liturgical ordinances. Israel's story was being consummated in the new Passover, fulfilled in his person by His life and death on the cross. The only way to convey the power of this monumental revelation is by the re-enactment of a new ritual in the partaking of bread and wine.

To properly capture the imagination, provoking reverence and spiritual awareness in the handling of things sacred, it is often necessary to formalize the oversight of the sublime with the administration of symbolic rites. By arranging meaning in ritual, we avoid the danger of treating the valuable as common, preventing our human weakness from treating the eternal as ordinary. In fact, when something truly inexplicable and indescribable needs to be expressed, we always lean on the aid of symbolic actions, which help us capture experiences that are beyond human comprehension[34]. How are we supposed to uphold the cup that Jesus ordained to be proclaimed as His blood of the new covenant? Our high priest established that our attitude should be one of gratitude, responding to God's divine action with the giving of thanks. What should be the perception of the elements of bread and wine that are shared as the meal of the kingdom at the table of communion? These elements should be viewed and received as consecrated food, given for the divine nourishment of the resurrected life of the believer. We ought to partake of communion as if consuming the new creation, invoking and conferring a special blessing upon the bread and wine following the priestly pattern illustrated by our Lord in the breaking of bread. The taking and eating in remembrance of Him is obviously not normal dining; it should be followed in a particular manner of introspection, with the distinctive format of a reverential protocol. The celebration of Passover was the backdrop of awareness in this community meal, signifying that a solemn convocation is at work behind all the activities of the gathered disciples. The Lord's Supper was instituted and officiated by the spiritual authority of the Lord himself, and it was prepared and designated for a targeted audience; namely, the Messiah's followers. We see in these events all the elements of a solemn rite being invoked at the communion table; it was conducted at a holy time, for a consecrated people, with some specific sacred actions designed to convey a redemptive meaning. The breaking of the bread, the blessing of the cup, the giving of thanks, the singing of a hymn—it was all pointing forward to the guidelines of a new order and procedure of worship that future generations were to observe and follow. A frequently ignored feature of the Lord's table is Jesus' washing of the disciples' feet, and another is His priestly prayer conducted after the Passover meal. Both actions, in

---

[34] As a man kneeling to give a ring to his future wife, or a crowd standing with hands on chests to honor a flag, or a moment of silence in memory of a special person.

the gospel of John, should also be understood as ceremonial activities intricately related to the rite of priestly requirements, designed for the participation of the Lord's table. Notice Biblical parallelism involved in some descriptions of the events, prior to and after the breaking of the bread with the Lord's disciples.

## *Priestly Parallelism*

| | |
|---|---|
| God gave the Levites to Aaron, the high priest, as a gift.[35] | God gave the disciples to Jesus as our new high priest.[36] |
| The high priest pronounced the holy name of God in the most holy place. | Jesus teaches and reveals to His disciples the divine name of God and the true character of His nature.[37] |
| The priestly lineage is consecrated for service by rituals of purification[38]. | The disciples are purified and ordained by the word of Jesus, and his example of humility illustrated in the washing of their feet. |
| The priesthood is a representation of God to the people, to unified divinity with humanity. | Jesus prayed that they all may be one as the Father in Him and Him in the Father.[39] |
| The priests were separated and sanctified to participate at the table, which included bread and wine. | The disciples were chosen and ordained to sit at the table of Jesus, to partake of His body and blood. |
| The aim of the high priest was to apprehend the glory of God in the holy of holies. | Jesus said to His Father, "The glory you have given me I have given to them, and I pray that they may see my glory."[40] |

---

[35] Numbers 8:19, Numbers 3:9.
[36] John 17:6.
[37] John 17:6, 12, 26.
[38] Numbers 8:7, Leviticus 8:6, John 17:17, 19, John 15:3, John 13:10.
[39] John 17:21-23.
[40] John 17:24, Leviticus 9:22-24.

# 2

# The Lord's Vision and Heart
# for Communion

## *The Main and Most Neglected Issue*

In many ways, this chapter is the most important in the book, because it plainly states the primary meaning and significance of communion. It also presents what I have discovered is the most challenging aspect of the Lord's Supper for many people. Even though what we are about to discuss is not complicated or sophisticated, many believers strongly resist the simplicity of embracing the true heart and vision of the Lord for communion. What is this elemental and basic truth of communion that so many struggle to apprehend? Here it is in the words of the Lord Himself:

> *"So now I am giving you a new commandment: Love each other. Just as I have loved you, you should love each other." (John 13:34 NLT)*

Not very exciting, right? Perhaps you will agree with me that it sounds too simplistic. Yet why is it so difficult to fulfill this commandment? We will soon discover that even though this instruction may look rudimentary, this is only because we are not engaging seriously with the profound complexity of our human condition. In the progression from Abraham to Moses, we see how sacrifices transitioned from

17

the patriarchal model of family to the national format of a collective consciousness. That was God's dealing with the people as a unit, training the nation to understand themselves in relation to God within the context of their connections with each other as a whole. The entirety of the sacrificial system was instituted to address the many dimensions of connectedness between the land, the people, and their God. Why does God remain hidden behind those curtains in the tabernacle of Moses? God revealed through His law during the wilderness wanderings that the human heart is by nature apathetic, indifferent, stubborn, and deceitfully wicked. Through the people of Israel, God showed us clearly how deep is our insufficiency and insensitivity to His presence, and how distant our heart is from His heart[41]. The tent dwellings and wilderness journeying was all about reducing life to the purest and simplest possible state—only eating manna and drinking pure water, focusing intensely and exclusively on the most basic purpose of all existence, which is knowing the presence of God and learning how to love Him in communion with others. The tabernacle adventure was the equivalent of going out camping on a date with someone you love, removing all distractions to spend quality time bonding together, soul searching and knowing each other intimately. The purpose of this camping trip was basically to test and expose the hidden things inside the people's hearts.

In the wilderness tabernacle, God demonstrated to humanity how closed we can really be to the experience of true intimacy and an authentic relationship in genuine worship. It's as if God was telling Israel, "I can see you are not really interested in getting to know me, you are only interested in the other nations seeing that I am with you. I can tell that you don't enjoy being alone with me. I am not enough for you to be satisfied, you always want to know what else you can get out of me to feed your lustful desires. I know you don't want a real relationship with me and I am going to prove it to you. Let's go out camping, just you and me alone in the wilderness!"

---

[41] Psalms 106:14-27, Deuteronomy 8:2-5, 1 Corinthians 10:1-11.

God moved the scenery for his glory from the garden to the desert by designing a little Eden in the midst of the wilderness. Back in paradise, surrounded by life, beauty, and delight they coveted the forbidden fruit. Now in the desert, surrounded by the absence of life in desolation, they should desire the return to the tree of life. This was like an exchange of trees; remember that in the Garden, the tree of life was accessible, while the dangerous tree of knowledge was prohibited. Now, with the knowledge of good and evil everywhere, perhaps we would have enough of its repercussions to instead start craving the inaccessible tree of life, which represents our eternal communion with God. What was unappreciated, undervalued and taken for granted in Eden must now be valued for its true worth and preciousness on the journey to the promised land. In Eden, the environment full of glory, beauty, and delight did not make the sacrifice of rejecting the knowledge of good and evil worth it to Adam and Eve. Now in the desert, the place that represents the consequences of death and decay from partaking of the forbidden fruit, perhaps human hearts will be provoked to abandon all things temporal for the only eternal thing that truly matters in life. *The longing of God to dwell in the midst of His people is illustrated in this tabernacle of fellowship, where the glory takes residence in worship, and the way to the tree of life that was guarded by cherubim is symbolically open in the Holy of Holies.*

The nation united in the sacrifices of the tabernacle and the people represented in the service of the priesthood created awareness of the importance of belonging to a community where they all expressed their unison before the presence of God. When the priests were eating and drinking around the table of show bread, symbolically the whole nation was dining with God, as it was represented by the twelve loaves of bread. As the high priest was beholding the glory of the Lord in the Holy of Holies, the entire worship of the twelve tribes of Israel was embodied in this one man, who materialized humanity to God and God to humanity. The format of tabernacle worship represented the harmony between the human and the divine. The heart of the Lord was to have one people, one temple, and one worship united under one God. The manna outside the tabernacle that the people needed to prepare every day forced the nation to reflect on how God was their sustenance and nourishment. The priests themselves prepared special bread with wine to be presented in the presence of the Lord as a fragrant offering as they were dining with God in the holy place. Even inside the Holy of Holies, there was a memorial of the supernatural manna from heaven that never grew old, representing the eternal nature of the true heavenly communion that God provided for His people. Therefore, we can see how the entirety of the wilderness experience was a prophetic picture of the heart and vision of the Lord for the unity of His people. Not only partaking of the bread from heaven together, but becoming one with Him as they were consecrated in His presence that was the tabernacle in their midst. When the Scriptures state that the word became flesh and pitched a tent among us, that is an allusion to that wilderness tabernacle of communion. That is why it immediately is followed with the statement, "And we beheld His glory as the only begotten of the Father, full of grace and truth." Imagine how enormous the desire of God must have been to live among us that He actually chose to forever become one of us in His Son. In His broken body and in the shedding of His precious blood, we are offered the opportunity to be united with the Son of God, becoming more fully and truly human. *The whole of divinity was seen in the fullness of humanity; therefore, we would never completely experience the divine until first we discovered how to become truly human.* Our present fallen condition does not allow us to genuinely participate in His eternal love, and that is why we reject Him at the table even when He appears with open arms, embracing us in His own humanity.

## Trouble in Paradise

Almost from the very moment the project of communion with God started in the desert, just like in the Garden of Eden, the human heart began to exert resistance against it. Rebellion against Moses, complaining in opposition to Aaron, and defiance in general towards God festered in the camp. To despise someone in leadership whose entire life is designed to sacrifice in love for your benefit helps us comprehend the dysfunction of the human condition. The people of God repudiated the servitude of Moses, yet celebrated the autocracy of Pharaoh, perhaps because secretly they admired the tyranny of the dictator, while simultaneously they resented the humility and love that was exemplified in the life of their deliverer. In other words, we would rather follow the pride of life in becoming a god unto ourselves than pay the price of transformation required to represent a loving servant. Pharaoh illustrates how the fruit of the knowledge of good and evil is to become a god, determining outcomes, shaping destiny, creating our own reality, and sitting in the seat of judgement to establish our own rules and laws. The law of Moses, broken at the feet of Mount Sinai at the sight of the idolatry of Israel, was all about exposing the hindrances to our unity with God, caused by the egotistical God complex buried deep within our sinful nature. We don't know how to properly honor and respect the line of distinction between the holy and the profane; therefore, we distort the image of the creator by not allowing Him to reveal who He truly is in our lives. *There can never be any potential for a relationship if there is not at least first an acknowledgement of the sacredness of others, beginning with the presence of God Himself.*

We asked before why God remains hidden behind the curtain; we wondered previously why it is so hard to love each other. We have here our answer in the broken law of Moses; this revelation shows clearly the fully developed fruit of the knowledge of good and evil in all of us. Since we have become like a god, governing our thoughts and imagination, we create our own fictional world of appearances where we set the boundaries of our perspective. We are now irreverent, unfaithful idolaters that deceive ourselves into coveting what is not ours and resent secretly the reality of God and others, pretending none of them are relevant to our existence. Believe it or not, none of this is as bad as the fact that many of us have a problem accepting or even considering that any of these descriptions are an accurate portrait of who we really are. It is a challenge just getting us to the mental place of considering the possibility that God is right about us when he speaks about our sinfulness, exposing us from behind the veil. Loving each other? We don't even know what love is! Loving each other as he loved us; that is literally a double impossibility! *If we desire to truly look into God's eyes, we must first allow His Spirit to give us faces He can gaze upon.* The marred image of God in us needs restoration, and it begins with a recognition of its decadent and perverse degeneration. Jesus, the ultimate son of man, the faithful and truthful Israelite, was broken at the sacramental table not only to unite mankind to God but to restore our humanity and to demonstrate the true interrelated nature of our existence. In our fallen condition, we think love is tolerance without accountability and pursue freedom at all costs with no regards to the responsibility of such privilege. We elevate above all else the pleasures of self-preservation and ignore the convictions that serve the interest of the collective, greater good. Communion is the challenge to sustain the tension of not allowing our liberty to become anarchy and protecting our love from falling victim to the repressive. This task is too large for mere men, with our frailty and weaknesses, and that is why God has dealt with it Himself through the human and divine intercession of our heavenly high priest. Jesus' priestly ministry is to reveal to us who we really are, healing, restoring, and addressing the unknown secrets and traumas hidden inside our fallen and broken condition. Now, perhaps, we get a glimpse of why this vision for unity and love in the Lord's Supper is so difficult for believers to understand; we haven't even scratched its surface.

## The Bread Through the Community's Eyes

Often, the overlooked secret of the church's distinctive identity is the particular lifestyle of unity and kinship that the disciples lived, learned directly from the experience of partaking communion with Christ. The breaking of bread, while it was officially sanctioned at Passover, was previously prominent in Jesus' ministry, even used often as a source of miraculous provision within their cult gatherings. The disciples saw the practice of blessing the breaking of bread as a symbol of their shared life of togetherness and closeness as a spiritual family. When Jesus said, "If you don't eat my flesh and drink my blood, you have no life in you," that was an aphorism referring to the policy of commonality that was shared within their loyal membership[42]. They were all fully invested in Jesus' vision of community, and that literally meant leaving all things behind to live full-time with Him as part of His sacred household[43]. For the disciples, this was like following a new Moses, experiencing a new exodus, living in fellowship with a new tabernacle and partaking of the new manna from heaven that returned humanity back to the lost glory of Eden[44]. It is interesting how the forty days of Jesus fasting in the desert parallel not only the forty years of testing of Israel in the wilderness, but also follow the pattern of devotion illustrated in the Lord's Prayer that is to be observed by the disciples.[45]

Our entire Christian pilgrimage can be understood as journeying in prayer through a spiritual wilderness with the challenge of learning authentic worship, being sustained by the true manna from heaven, and becoming a community that defeats the enemy by being united in the loving example of our Messiah.[46] The Lord's prayer itself urges to belong to an interdependent, undivided, reciprocal entity that sees itself within the confines of a congenial bond concerned for the destiny of all its members. We can see how, in light of these observations,

---

[42] Luke 14:25-33, Matthew 16:24-25, Mark 10:21, 28.

[43] Matthew 12:48-50.

[44] The John 6:26-68 discourse of eating the flesh and blood of Jesus is framed and contrasted within the context of the wilderness wanderings of Israel following Moses, and the nature of the manna from heaven that Jesus gives to His disciples.

[45] In the Lord's prayer, the phrase "lead us not into temptation but deliver us from evil" mirrors the experiences of the wilderness wanderings of Israel, and the desert temptations of Christ. The temptation of turning stones into bread parallels the petition in the Lord's prayer to ask every day for our daily bread, and it also contrasts the failure of Israel of not living by bread alone, not trusting in every word that proceeds out of the mouth of God. In the temptation of Christ, being offered all the kingdoms of the world if he bows down and pays homage to Satan resembles the focus of worship in the entirety of the Lord's Prayer; "Hallowed be your name, for thine is the kingdom and the glory and the power forever." This was also what was originally delivered to Israel as the foundation of their faith; they shall worship the Lord their God, and Him only shall they serve.

[46] Perhaps this is also why Jesus stayed with the disciples for a period of forty days after the resurrection, illustrating and teaching about the tabernacle life of the Kingdom of God on Earth (Acts 1:3).

the statements of verses like Acts 2:42-47- Acts 4:32-35 become more distinctively illuminated. By living together as the Messiah's body, the believers were simply preserving and continuing the learned behavior assimilated by the doctrines and practices of the Lord Himself.

> *"All the believers devoted themselves to the apostles' teaching, and to fellowship, and to sharing in meals (including the Lord's Supper), and to prayer. A deep sense of awe came over them all, and the apostles performed many miraculous signs and wonders. And all the believers met together in one place and shared everything they had. They sold their property and possessions and shared the money with those in need. They worshiped together at the Temple each day, met in homes for the Lord's Supper, and shared their meals with great joy and generosity—all the while praising God and enjoying the goodwill of all the people. And each day the Lord added to their fellowship those who were being saved."* (Acts of the Apostles 2:42-47 NLT)

> *"All the believers were united in heart and mind. And they felt that what they owned was not their own, so they shared everything they had. The apostles testified powerfully to the resurrection of the Lord Jesus, and God's great blessing was upon them all. There were no needy people among them, because those who owned land or houses would sell them and bring the money to the apostles to give to those in need."* (Acts of the Apostles 4:32-35 NLT)

The true Passover has already come; they are all leaving Egypt behind, and they are celebrating the inauguration of the Kingdom inside them like Israel in the desert, camping around the Glory of the Lord that is now concentrated in the celebration of the bread and the wine of communion. Interestingly, if the Passover feast was consummated in the liberation through the Lord's death, and Pentecost was fulfilled in birthing a new people in the coming of the Spirit, then what else is left to do for the people of God but to live together in unity celebrating tabernacles?

When Jesus said to His disciples, this is my body broken for you, that was a very real and personal declaration that modeled the devotion, commitment, and allegiance demonstrated to His company of brothers. At the moment the cup of salvation was presented as the blood of the new covenant, they undoubtedly remembered the complete abandonment and passion that the Lord expended on the cross when he loved them extravagantly to the very end. Unity with Christ through the sacraments couldn't be interpreted by the community in any other fashion than complete assimilation of the heart and vision of the Lord for communion among all of His members. The challenge is now to bring others to experience, through our vulnerability and openness, the loyalty and security God cherishes for each one of us as part of His corporal body. No wonder for many today the Lord's Supper is empty of meaning and significance; this rite goes against all the social conventions that we have grown so accustomed to within our consumerist society. The incarnation is all about God taking upon Himself the very human life that so many seek to avoid; the Son of God embraced the actuality of His natural environment, growing and learning from all His earthly interactions with His peers. How can any of us sit at the Lord's table with people we don't even know or care to understand? How can we attempt to celebrate something that contradicts everything for which we currently stand as a secular society? If we are unwilling or uninterested in allowing the lives of others to become relevant or significant to who we are as believers, then it will eventually become impossible to partake of the true power and meaning of the Lord's Supper for today.

In the gospel of John, the famous confession of Peter that Jesus is the Messiah, the Son of the living God, is interpreted within the bread of life discourse of eating the flesh and drinking the blood of the Son of God to have eternal life[47]. This is relevant to the understanding that for John, membership into the people of the Messiah is not only about declaring the truth of His identity, but also about completely identifying with His sacrifice and vision and partaking of His love as a faithful community. If John is truly making allusion to the rite of the Lord's

---

[47] John 6:68-69, Matthew 16:16.

Supper in the bread from heaven discourse, then in order to continually drink His blood and eat His flesh, we need to have faithful alliance to His sacramental presence, which belongs to the covenant people of God. Peter's journey across the gospel of John shows him progressively following the example of Christ into conformity to His death and sacrifice of love, even reaching the testimony of glorifying God by succeeding totally in His footsteps. Eventually the full scope of partaking of Jesus' flesh and blood gets unveiled, in the process of maturation of Peter after enduring brokenness, and surrendering to Christ's vision for commonality and oneness with Him. The resurrected, glorified body of the Messiah transformed believers into a new living organism, in which Christ shares His grace and essence with all those who receive and believe in His vision for spiritual consolidation. Peter Himself seems to be confronted with this realization when he is commissioned to exhibit his love for Jesus in the duty of caring and attending for the spiritual wellbeing of all God's people. The way Peter will show his loyalty to the Lord is by his attention to his flock. Loving the Lord's congregation by nurturing the sheep becomes the means by which his conformity to Christ's image is ultimately achieved.

*"Simon Peter asked, 'Lord, where are you going?' And Jesus replied, 'You can't go with me now, but you will follow me later.'" (John 13:36 NLT)*

The Lord is saying to Peter that eventually he will live consumed with giving the example of Christ's sacramental life to others.

*"Jesus said this to let him know by what kind of death he would glorify God. Then Jesus told him, 'Follow me.'" (John 21:19 NLT)*

# 3

# Communion: The Announcement of the Kingdom

*Proclamation of Emancipation*

Everything we have studied so far is fundamentally enclosed and confined to the life of the Church. The sharing in the fellowship table of the Lord operates as a channel for the preservation of the worship, vision, and life for the community as God's people. But there is another dimension to the Lord's Supper that often gets neglected by those who partake of the elements of holy communion. We are not just looking into ourselves and our relationship with God as we enjoy our sacred meal together. There is also a decree that we are pronouncing to the powers of this world: we are notifying this present age that God's Kingdom has arrived in our hearts and lives when we partake of the sacramental presence of Christ. Perhaps the blurring of this truth has come as a result of isolating the Lord's Supper from its direct connection to the cross and its meaning in the kingdom. The bread and the wine can be understood as the body and blood of the Messiah, making the sacrament of the Lord's table and the royal coronation of the Lord at the cross permanently inseparable. In fact, the eating of the broken bread and the drinking of the new covenant cup were instituted and designed to actualize and enforce the significance of the Lord's death towards our earthly lives. Notice how the scripture makes mention of these facts by attesting to the outward impact of properly commemorating the Lord's table:

*"For as often as you eat this bread and drink the cup, you proclaim the Lord's death until he comes" (1 Corinthians 11:26).*

This small phrase is loaded with substantial meaning that needs careful unpacking. For example, the statement, "We proclaim the Lord's death" is attesting to a monumental event that requires a response, since it involves literally everything that exists within creation. The word "proclaim" in the New Testament always carries the connotation of referencing ubiquitous truths that need particular emphasis[48]. This word is reserved exclusively to highlight climactic and momentous occurrences, with important and broad ramifications for those involved. The Lord's death is not an insignificant, unfortunate accident of history; it is the decisive moment in time when judgment was pronounced upon the forces of darkness, removing the destructive influence of death, sin, and decay from its illegitimate authority. We have normalized and standardized the cross as a symbol of victory, but why is that? There is nothing glamorous in death by crucifixion; really, it was a shameful and horrifying punishment designed to discourage rebellion against the established authority. Since it was a common symbol in the first century of defeat and brutality, how did it come to serve as a picture of triumph? The answer is found in who was dying on the tree, and the reasons for His willful enduring of such suffering. When God wanted to openly and publicly reveal to all creation who He is, in all of His glory and power, He sent His Son to die on the cross. It was a subversive event that reverses common expectations, destroys human and divine conventions, and transforms the complete perspective of the true order of creation.

By eating and drinking as a community that belongs to the Messiah, we consume of that divine event on the cross, where His Kingdom was

---

[48] Acts 4:2, 13:5, 13:38, 15:36, 16:17, 16:21, 17:3, 17:13, 26:23, Romans 1:8, 1 Corinthians 2:1, 9:14, Colossians 1:28.

launched towards all that exists. We are figuratively and practically making known to our minds and hearts His victory until He returns. That returning of the Lord is intricately connected to His death, since it is nothing less than the complete manifestation of all that was purchased and conquered through the broken body of the Messiah on the cross. Therefore, until all that was accomplished on the cross gets fully revealed by the royal appearance of the King Himself, we are called to be faithful stewards and witnesses of those divine realities by announcing them through the sacrament of communion. The scripture clearly presents the counteraction involved at the glorification of the Lord at the cross. His death is a multifaceted event that requires proclamation, as it concurrently addresses God, mankind, and all the inhabitants of the spiritual realm.

*"Since the children have flesh and blood, he too shared in their humanity so that by his death he might break the power of him who holds the power of death that is, the devil." (Hebrews 2:14)*

*"Now is the time for judgment on this world; now the prince of this world will be driven out. And I, when I am lifted up from the earth, will draw all people to myself." (John 12:31)*

He said this to show the kind of death he was going to die.

*"Having canceled the charge of our legal indebtedness, which stood against us and condemned us; he has taken it away, nailing it to the cross. And having disarmed the powers and authorities, he made a public spectacle of them, triumphing over them by the cross." (Colossians 2:14–15)*

*"For in him all things were created: things in heaven and on earth, visible and invisible, whether thrones or powers or rulers or authorities; all things have been created through him and for him. He is before all things, and in him all things hold together. For God was pleased to have all his fullness dwell in him, and*

> *through him to reconcile to himself all things, whether things on earth or things in heaven, by making peace through his blood, shed on the cross." (Colossians 1:16-20)*

Reminding the invisible forces of this world that their defeat transpired through the Lord's death apparently releases the mysterious atmosphere of new creation, and we do so when we dramatize the redemptive sufferings of Christ in the breaking of the bread. In the moment we announce a new dispensation of glory and propitiation in the blood of the new covenant, we partake of the cup of our salvation as a supernatural manifesto that gets delivered to the spiritual realm, serving notice to the powers of darkness that their influence over our lives has been forever broken. In the book of Revelation, when the veil to the realm of the Spirit is opened, the image of the Lamb enthroned is described and the triumph of His sacrifice accomplished by His blood is witnessed, as is being celebrated in the heavens. We are united to that heavenly worship, understanding that our natural condition is not the ultimate state of reality when we partake of the body and blood of the Lamb of God. Our heavenly High Priest is making intercession for us so that all that is true of Him will become true of us on Earth. Even if we suffer on Earth, just like the Lamb on the cross, we overcome through His death, and we emulate His victorious sacrifice when persecuted or challenged.

The message of the cross and its proclamation as a sacramental meal conveys a message to our fallen world, that they must learn how to assimilate the true nature of the kingdom of God. The broken body of the Messiah says to the rulers and authorities in the invisible realm that they must change the way they perceive things, because the order of creation as it was previously known has already been prosecuted. The Biblical worldview presents a spiritual conflict that has reached a climax in the coming of Christ. In the life, death, and resurrection of Jesus, the problem of evil and the unfinished project of creation has finally been addressed to progressively reach divine resolution and miraculous restoration. We are called to eat together as a community, where the social labels and stigmas that once defined and separated us have been forever transformed and removed. The very act of commemorating the Lord's Supper with His vision for unity and reconciliation establishes a spiritual precedent, repelling the forces of darkness that try to manipulate our way of thinking within the systems of control of this fallen world. Let's take a moment to examine some of the ways in which the meal of the kingdom makes proclamation to the dark powers of their inadequacy and defeat.

## Message Conveyed to the Powers and Rulers of this Present Age

*1. The nature of God is superior to all displays of self-aggrandizing dominance.* In the Biblical narrative, there is an account of a rebellion that took place in the heavenly realm, where divine beings opposed and conspired against the sovereign authority of the creator God. They took the delegated authority and influence that was conferred upon them and began to corrupt their character and influence, promoting the arrogance and vanity of pride[49]. What better way to accentuate their failure and condemnation than to expose through the cross their very means of control as powerless? The crucifixion is not only the triumph of humility and lowliness over power and control, it is also the rendering of prepotency as flawed and deficient for all authorities but God. There is a new and better way of living and operating within our structures of leadership and administration. The government of God is illustrated at His kingdom table, where one family with new hearts and new minds follows the servant model of Messiah, esteeming others above themselves in the loving nature of Christ's humility and service.

In a world where people predominantly seek to gain positions and prestige through ostentatious conduct, God's people shine bright in their transformed character by willingly renouncing their social stature and reputation to adopt the modesty of self-sacrificial obedience of the Son of God. The claim of the forces of darkness is that we have

---

[49] Psalms 82, 89:6-8, Deuteronomy 4:19, 32:8-9, Daniel 4:17, 7:9, Zachariah 3:1, Job 1:6, Job 2:1, Isaiah 14, Ezekiel 28.

bowed our knee in reverence before the allure of the vanity of appearances, because our affection is towards the desires for self-gratification behind the power structures of our perverse generation[50]. But when the Church as royal priesthood and the holy nation choose to deny their rights, sacrificing all privileges without expecting anything in return, then the sacrament of communion becomes a witness of the victory of the cross over the vanity and pride of life advertised by the powers of darkness. Remember, Passover was originally a subversive meal that not only recalled freedom from the gods of Egypt, but also looked forward towards future liberation from all additional foreign powers. Interpreting governments, empires, and even kings as representations of invisible forces was a common perspective in ancient times. Therefore, Passover as well as the Lord's Supper was an act of defiance that undermined the current forces in charge of their right to rule both spiritually and socially over the hearts and minds of the community. The sacred meal at the church gathering not only challenged the current powers that controlled the world, it also exposed how the humility and purity of the true king of the universe destroyed all their hostility and aggression by His meekness at the cross. At the center of Satan's (the divine rebel's) opposition to God was his pride and condescension. For us at the heart of our Christian celebration of the Eucharist is the submissiveness of the Son of God, and our imitation of His servitude and self-emptying.

> *"Then make me truly happy by agreeing wholeheartedly with each other, loving one another, and working together with one mind and purpose. Don't be selfish; don't try to impress others. Be humble, thinking of others as better than yourselves. Don't look out only for your own interests, but take an interest in others, too. You must have the same attitude that Christ Jesus had. Though he was God, he did not think of equality with God as something to cling to. Instead, he gave up his divine privileges; he took the humble position of a slave and was born as a human being. When he appeared in human form, he humbled himself in obedience to God*

---

[50] Luke 4:1-13.

*and died a criminal's death on a cross. Therefore, God elevated him to the place of highest honor and gave him the name above all other names, that at the name of Jesus every knee should bow, in heaven and on earth and under the earth, and every tongue declare that Jesus Christ is Lord, to the glory of God the Father."*
*(Philippians 2:2-11 NLT)*

*2. The markers and classifications that used to define us can no longer determine our true value and identity.* The dark forces of evil divided mankind, isolating people into unchanging, established designations. The order of civil duties and the classifications of economic status governed the way workers, neighbors, and citizens among the nations of the world interacted. In the Greco-Roman system, this inequity and disparity was associated with the gods and their favoritism towards the privileged and powerful. In this Hellenistic setting, banquets were conducted as spiritual enterprises designed to reinforce the divine mandate of the Empire to rule the world and keep citizens in their assigned roles[51]. Every member of the social structure was reminded of their allotted destiny and status by where they sat at the banquet table, and with whom they were allowed to dine. To be free from such constrictions must have felt like an impossible aspiration, only possible perhaps by some divine or miraculous intervention. Jesus' kingdom banquet reverses all those social and ethical expectations, challenging the boundaries of ethnic and cultural distinctions. No one was Jew or Gentile, male or female, slave or free at the Lord's fellowship meal. The meal of the Kingdom is a participation of the glory of the cross; therefore, whatever was released in that divine transaction gets transferred to us by the worshipful consumption of the elements of communion. Jesus abolished the old order of things on the cross, and now has given us a new identity in His resurrected body, of which we partake in the bread and wine.

*"As for me, may I never boast about anything except the cross of our Lord Jesus Christ. Because of that cross, my interest in this*

---

[51] *Subversive Meals*, chapter 3, 2013. PickWick publications by: R. Alan Streett.

*world has been crucified, and the world's interest in me has also died." (Galatians 6:14 NLT)*

The Bible speaks of the triumph of the Messiah over the forces of darkness, depicting how the bondage of nations to regional deities has finally been overthrown. The seating of the Messiah at the same dinner table with Gentiles, minorities, destitute people, orphans, widows, and other marginalized groups was an undeniable witness to the principalities and powers that their time was up, and that the inauguration of the Kingdom of God had arrived on Earth.

*"And they sang a new song with these words: 'You are worthy to take the scroll and break its seals and open it. For you were slaughtered, and your blood has ransomed people for God from every tribe and language and people and nation. And you have caused them to become a Kingdom of priests for our God. And they will reign on the Earth.'" (Revelation 5:9–10 NLT)*

*"Then there was war in heaven. Michael and his angels fought against the dragon and his angels. And the dragon lost the battle, and he and his angels were forced out of heaven. This great dragon—the ancient serpent called the devil, or Satan, the one deceiving the whole world—was thrown down to the earth with all his angels. Then I heard a loud voice shouting across the heavens, 'It has come at last— salvation and power and the Kingdom of our God, and the authority of his Christ. For the accuser of our brothers and sisters has been thrown down to earth—the one who accuses them before our God day and night. And they have defeated him by the blood of the Lamb and by their testimony. And they did not love their lives so much that they were afraid to die." (Revelation 12:7–11 NLT)*

The failure of our Christian communities is evident when the only thing that unites us is our carnal, worldly, or cultural identities. We should not allow ourselves to be separated by denominational lines, trivial superficial differences in styles of worship, or preferences in religious traditions.

When division, strife, and jealousy try to separate the community of believers, the Lord's Supper testifies of surrendering to God's will and leaving the ultimate judgment and justice of things in the hands of our King who offered us a kingdom of forgiveness. That is what is celebrated at the Eucharist: supernatural release and healing from all spiritual offenses, and deliverance from the forces of destruction that seek to enslave and manipulate us into spiritual bondage. The sacramental church should be multicultural, displaying unity and love among its members.

> *"Those who belong to Christ Jesus have nailed the passions and desires of their sinful nature to his cross and crucified them there."* *(Galatians 5:24 NLT)*

> *"We know that our old sinful selves were crucified with Christ so that sin might lose its power in our lives. We are no longer slaves to sin." (Romans 6:6 NLT)*

3. *The aim of all existence is now consummated in the passion and intimacy found in the love of the Son of God.* There is a powerful drama being described throughout the Bible, in which evil forces have sabotaged the sanctified union between God and humanity by the means of idolatry and deception. The original joining of heaven and Earth is articulated prophetically in scripture, in terms of a romantic relationship of a husband with his wife. The fallout and separation from the heart of true worship to the creator God is characterized as the equivalent of committing spiritual adultery. Not only that, but all of history is Biblically described as the prophetic movement towards the climactic event of the Marriage Supper of the Lamb. The aim of the rebellious powers that oppose God from the very beginning of time has been to seduce and

pervert human affection away from seeking covenant intimacy with the creator[52]. Paul writes to the Corinthians:

> *"You cannot drink from the cup of the Lord and from the cup of demons, too. You cannot eat at the Lord's Table and at the table of demons, too."*

> *"What? Do we dare to rouse the Lord's jealousy? Do you think we are stronger than he is?"*

It is interesting that one of the origins of perversion in the scriptures is attributed to a portion of the divine beings that mingle with the daughters of men[53], as if mimicking the holy matrimony between man and woman. These divine rebels seem to desire for themselves what they see that God has preordained for the human race. This often hushed event of Genesis 6 looks literally like an attempt to sabotage the miracle of the incarnation[54]. By mixing the races and producing a hybrid genealogy, there won't be any room for the promised seed of the woman predicted in the prophecy of Genesis 3. One of the most ancient traditions of the origin of demons is that they were the disembodied spirits of the hybrid race of giants that came from the illegitimate union between the

---

[52] 2 Corinthians 11:3.
[53] Genesis 6:1-4. Apparently this is one of the main reasons the world was destroyed.
[54] Genesis 3:15, Romans 1:2-4.

sons of God and the daughters of men[55]. This tradition is significant, because when Paul says you cannot partake of the table of demons, he is indirectly bringing to mind this entire world of spiritual forces discharged into the world to prevent intimacy and covenant union with Christ. The cross, dramatized in our communal dining, goes beyond our intellectual persuasions. If we only rationalize philosophically the theological meaning of our congregational banquet, we have tragically missed the point of partaking of this meal. The sacramental presence of Christ is, at its core, a heart appeal that was designed to deeply move our entire being into the assimilation of Christ's passion.

*The scriptures are neither a manual for success nor a rulebook for the display of power. The Bible story is the passionate tale of sacrificial love in the eternal quest for intimate worship.*

---

[55] Job 26:5, Psalms 88:10, Proverbs 2:18, Proverbs 9:18, Proverbs 21:16, Isaiah 14:9, 11, 15, Isaiah 26:14, Isaiah 26:19. The word "Raphaim" (one of the giants' clans) in these verses was translated as "spirits" or "departed" ones. These verses, which associate the word "Raphaim" (giants) with Sheol (the place of the dead), could be one of the sources for the speculation that demons are disembodied spirits from the hybrid race of the Genesis 6 event, since giants were drowned during the flood and the divine beings of Genesis 6 were believed to be incarcerated in prisons of darkness (1 Peter 3:18, 2 Peter 2:4-5, 9, Jude 1:6-7). The name Raphaim began to be associated with the terrors of death and the torments of the place of the departed evil spirits reserved for judgement. When people saw afflicted souls tormented by evil spirits, one can imagine that it reminded them of the unholy mixture that produced strange spiritual forces that, having lost their habitation during the flood, now have no place for rest in their existence other than imposing themselves unto our flesh. In the New Testament, demons are seen as having knowledge of being sent into the Abyss (Luke 8:3); this looks as if they recalled the divine judgements of Genesis 6. In that same passage, the demons requested to be sent into pigs, as if seeking not to lose embodiment—something that is also recalled in Luke 11:24-26. In Luke 11:24, the demons are described as if they seek to avoid water at all costs, preferring dry desert places. When the demons enter the pigs in Luke 8:33, they run into water and drown. Pigs are known to be good swimmers; what is it about demons that causes animals that are comfortable in water to suddenly frantically panic and end up drowning? Could Luke in this story be drawing a picture to show how demons are tormented by water, reminding them of how originally they lost their embodiment in the flood?

We are supposed to announce to the powers we are in covenant, and all their perversions have been defeated. Not only have we betrothed our God, we are already worshiping Him with the passion of the world to come releasing His divine nature at His table. The Lord is displaying in front of the fallen rebels the love, loyalty, and intimacy of His bride[56]. One of the ways of understanding communion is the Jewish custom of celebrating the engagement of a couple with a cup of wine. If fallen creatures are assigned the destruction of God's love story, then we as the Lord's bride should be on alert to rekindle the fire of passion during our liturgical worship.

*4. The new creation is inaugurated in God's people progressing and, paradoxically, influencing all things.* Rarely do we imagine our partaking of the Lord's Kingdom meal as an illustration of the heavenly realm, or the wisdom and glory of God on Earth. Often it is difficult to conceive our enjoyment of peace, love, faith, and hope as revelations to celestial beings of the eternal purposes of God fulfilled in the church[57]. The priestly ministry of Jesus is portrayed in the New Testament as one reigning in the midst of His enemies[58]. That is, in His suffering and death, our King was instrumental in birthing a new dispensation of grace that is still informing the invisible realm of the shortcomings of their previous administration over the earth. As sacramental people, our representing the Lord's scars faithfully as part of His eschatological body is a sign to the rulers and authorities of their defeat. We not only express our way of living as superior to the old order of creation, but our vision of unity and love consistently defeats every attempt of evil that tries to challenge the supremacy of the Kingdom of God in our hearts. We are not vindictive people, for in the cross we learn ultimate forgiveness. There is no room at the table for selfishness; the breaking of bread is all about self-emptying, becoming more united in our common humanity. We resist the temptation to dominate or impose our will, for in the shedding of Jesus' blood the Son of God stated not my will, but *thy will* be done. We don't look at the present condition of things as the

---

[56] Psalms 23:5, Song of Solomon 1:2, 4.
[57] Ephesians 3:10-11.
[58] Psalms 110:1-3, 1 Corinthians 15:23-26.

ideal reality, because the cross is a lesson that glory, eternity, and true purpose is found in forsaking all temporal things to invest our legacy in God's future. In God's kingdom meal, we no longer are seduced by the allure of temporal superficialities; instead we recognize that success is elusive, deceptive, and relative to perspective, because it was Jesus who by losing all taught us how to truly gain everything.

## Avoiding the Deceptions of the Enemies of the Cross

There is a specific form to the Lord's Supper that, if altered or distorted, will dilute the overall impact and intention of the spiritual purpose of this rite. It is not enough to conduct a ritual routinely at our church meetings, and think that alone will inform the spiritual forces of darkness that Christ is the king over our lives. It seems that we have allowed many of our congregations to depart from a clear understanding of the way sacraments are supposed to function in the devotional experience of the believer. As a result, even the message of the cross and the revelation of the Kingdom banquet has become corrupted, resulting in a perversion that actually promotes the complete opposite of what the true heart of the gospel is really all about.

> *"For I have told you often before, and I say it again with tears in my eyes, that there are many whose conduct shows they are really enemies of the cross of Christ." (Philippians 3:18 NLT)*

1. *Those who teach to take advantage of Jesus, only seeing His sacrifice as a means to gain benefits and rewards.* Many times I hear ministers going into the celebration of the Eucharist as if they are about to cash in on a spiritual wish list. Modern Christians are so indoctrinated in false spirituality that they have been desensitized to the Faith, interpreting love as a simple pleasure that fills us with whims and avoids suffering. The cross is not only to admire what God did to benefit us, but also to follow the example of Jesus and imitate his sacrifice. These new attractive presentations of the gospel behave as though Jesus was a humanist. The presupposition is that the Lord has come for the prime objective

of wellness, for goodness' sake. But this was condemned by Jesus when he confronted Peter:

> *"Jesus turned to Peter and said, 'Get away from me, Satan! You are a dangerous trap to me. You are seeing things merely from a human point of view, not from God's.'" (Matthew 16:23 NLT)*

In this text we can see how the personification of evil is characterized by distortions of the perception of the cross.

*2. Those who distort the Christian devotion to an individualistic plane, privatizing spirituality and faith out of the context of the Christ-centered community.* It is very difficult to talk about accountability, submission, or doing life with others when many of our church structures are built to promote a system of the exploitation of others. Nevertheless, a lot of Christian activities are designed to advance the experience of spiritual narcissism, gathering us in a place to isolate our internal reflections about God according to each of our individualistic interpretations. I honestly don't see how any of these efforts will ever produce lasting change or the permanent fruit of Christlikeness in believers. This could be a very difficult pill to swallow, but the Bible is not designed for isolation. It was always from the beginning constructed, shaped, and preserved through and for the Lord's community. In the book of Revelation, Jesus is shown ministering to His Church. He knows where they are at in their geographic, economic, and cultural context. He knows what they are facing in their congregations with their errors and false teachers, and he knows all the specific challenges they must overcome. Yet He is still speaking to them all; He is still giving them a tailored message for each congregation and their leadership, and He is imparting to them a special grace, a unique measure of the Spirit in which they can all partake together. Our connection to the Father is through the priestly ministry of Jesus, and that experience is enjoyed in the power of the Spirit inside the context of the Lord's assembly. The Holy Spirit Himself is given for the communion, empowerment, and mission of the Church.

Therefore, anything we do that distorts this specific vision is opposing the purpose of Christ's death on the cross.

*3. Whoever attempts to commercialize grace and closeness to God, advertising it as a product to be sold in the marketplace of ideas.* So I am looking at a huge building on TV packed with thousands of people, and I tell a friend sitting next to me, "Look at that! Is that not an amazing church?" He looks back at me smiling and answers, "Yes, that's the best church money can buy!"

The best church money can buy:

- If you remove the salaries from its staff, you would lose the majority of its leadership to the next-highest bidder.

- Without the fancy building, the expensive sound system, and the state-of-the-art technology, 80% of the membership would decrease.

- They resolve everything by throwing money at problems, replacing pastoral care with social work, and creating the illusion of compassion by marketing faith and selling spirituality.

- With their million-dollar budget, they schedule celebrity preachers and famous artists that no other church can afford in order to increase their popularity, gaining more influence within the star-driven, ego-intoxicated gospel culture of today.

- They always remove all inconveniences, fix all difficulties, and create a comfortable experience for people that avoids testing their faith, eliminating the human challenges that create the potential for true spiritual growth.

- Their members reflect the vision of their church, constantly living for themselves and seeing others only as a means to reach their individual aspirations, pursuing the fulfillment of their personal goals at any cost.

- Their success is carefully measured by numbers, always evaluating the size of their bank accounts, the salary of their leadership, and the lifestyles of their members.

*4. Everyone who seeks to promote and exalt all the very things that God is trying to crucify in us, be it self, vanity, or the world.* Growing up in the church, I got accustomed to hearing messages of encouragement that sought to build people's self-esteem. Many of these well-intentioned sermons would emphasize success, ambition, and thriving over opposition. Perhaps the rationale behind this ministry spectacle is simply to expand the influence of the church's outreach. Or perhaps it is to create a new platform for Christianity, to help society find the principles and truths that could impact their minds and benefit their ways of life. While the motivation seems sincere, and the intention might be noble, the effects of this unholy mixture could be more problematic than profitable. We should all know by now that the answer to our decaying and corrupt culture is not better counseling or more practical advice, but a radical transformation of the heart, which is only possible by the power of a face-to-face encounter with God.

We've seen before how preachers turn into politicians, and psalmists transform themselves into artists. Always seeking greater stages and pursuing wider venues, they often end up losing more than they gained. Their gift is reduced to entertainment, and their grace is distorted into a commodity. Their delegated authority is demoted to personal opinion, and their vocational calling is turned into a professional, public career. When the salt loses its flavor, how can it be made salty again? It is no longer good for anything, except to be thrown out and trampled underfoot (Matthew 5:13).

Seeking to become relevant, we often pollute what makes us distinctive. Attempting to win the world, we end up losing our souls and compromising our integrity. As a minister, it is one thing to lust after the worldly ambitions of today's immoral culture. It is quite another thing to stoop so low as to promote that carnality inside your own ministry, endorsing and selling pseudospirituality within your Christian audience.

We are so confused and twisted today that now the world looks like the church and the church looks like the world. It is not accidental, nor peripheral, that the scriptures clearly admonish against friendship with the world, constituting it as enmity against God (James 4:4, 1 Thessalonians 5:22, 2 Corinthians 6:14-18). It looks to me like it's time that we go back and focus on our consecration, and reclaim afresh our true legacy of holiness and purity in the pulpit. Let's get the leaven out and see our lives rededicated to God in Spirit and in Truth once again.

# 4

# Transfigured Communion

## *The Fulfillment and Consummation of the Bread and Wine*

We have seen how Jesus understood the events of His death on the cross as part of His redemptive work for humanity, and also how God used the sacrifice of His Son as a weapon to judge and destroy all the evil powers that permeated the entire world. What we have examined so far is how God's Kingdom is being inaugurated in the very person of the Messiah, and how God is preserving and releasing His transformative glory and nature to us as we partake of the consecrated elements that are proclaimed as His body and blood of the new covenant. Part of the training of the disciples leading up to the events on the cross was opening their minds to the possibilities available to them in their connection with the Son of God. In the mountain of transfiguration, they saw the son of man coming in the Kingdom of God with power[59]. Even when Jesus had not gone to the cross yet, future events could be addressed, discussed, and experienced as already fulfilled[60]. One of the main emphases of this mountaintop revelation was to understand how

---

[59] Luke 9:28-36, 2 Peter 1:16-18, Matthew 16:28, Mark 9:1, Luke 9:27. This would mean that they somehow experienced the future glory of the second coming as a reality already accessible in the transfigured Jesus.

[60] Luke 9:31. If the second coming and the kingdom are experienced in the transfigured body, then that same body could bring that glory into the present and prepare us for that glorious future when encountered through the elements.

glory is hidden behind suffering[61]. *Divine perspective is the window by which we transcend outward appearances to discern heavenly realities.* They converse in glory on the mountain of revelation about things that, from an Earthly point of view, could not be comprehended. In the book of Luke, there are subtle parallels between this account and the road to Emmaus story, which takes place after the Resurrection[62]. Notice how on both occasions, Jesus is in the disciples' midst in a different form, yet the disciples are unable to see His true glory primarily because of a lack of revelation concerning His sacramental presence[63]. In both instances, the specific message of the cross is shared, a message which needed to be observed in order to understand what had been accomplished and fulfilled through the sufferings of the Messiah[64]. Jesus, in both accounts, alludes to the interlocking harmony of all salvation history, arguing that the law and prophets represented in the mountain by Moses and Elijah were consummated by Him. When Luke allegorically connects the mountain of transfiguration to the road to Emmaus, he is implying that both events should be interpreted together as instances in which observers struggle to see the fulfillment of the scriptures in front of their eyes because of the lack of divine perspective. Not only that, but perhaps more importantly, when the two events are paralleled together Luke could be cleverly describing what occurred on the mountain as the glorious illustration of what later is communicated at the table. This is almost like a theological course training on how to lead people into true intimacy with the glorified body of the risen Christ[65]. It is not obvious, and it is not apparent, to see Jesus clearly in all His glory. The finished work of the Messiah is introducing the future heirs of

---

[61] Luke 9:30-31.

[62] Luke 24:13-35.

[63] Luke 9:36, Luke 9:45, Matthew 17:9, Mark 9:10, Luke 24:16. Part of the problem with the disciples' interpretation of the transfiguration was that they didn't comprehend yet how the glory they witnessed was supposed to be acquired through the redemptive sufferings wrought in the glorified body of Christ.

[64] Luke 9:31,44, Luke 24:26.

[65] We need the whole narrative—the story of scripture pointing to a climax in Christ, the burning of the Holy Spirit in people's hearts, and all the ministry culminating in the sacramental breaking of the bread—to open the eyes to the reality of the kingdom of God.

the Kingdom to a new way of thinking and living, to escape Earthly paradigms and embrace the divine perspective of heaven on Earth. To truthfully discern Him for who He really is, you must see his divine presence everywhere, adjusting your spiritual lenses to the vantage point of the fulfillment of the scriptures in His person[66]. Perhaps most shocking of all is that the disciples' eyes were not fully opened until they participated in the breaking of the bread. Scriptures, prayers, miracles, visions, good preaching, and hearts burning were not enough; it all needed to come together in the transfiguration of the communion. This was an important lesson Christ was teaching His followers; He was basically implying, "If you aren't going to see me through the reality of new creation in word and sacrament, it's better that you don't see me at all. I will remain hidden, patiently talking to you from my transfigured perspective, even pretending I am a part of the unchanged world, nudging at your heart until you are able to see how all is coming together and being fulfilled in my person." All of history, creation, and even death are transformed in the redemptive work of Christ. The sermon never stops until we are finally ready to invite the King of glory into our house to dine with us at His Kingdom table.

*"As they sat down to eat, he took the bread and blessed it. Then he broke it and gave it to them. Suddenly, their eyes were opened, and they recognized him. And at that moment he disappeared!" (Luke 24:30-31 NLT)*

Did you catch that? You don't need to see Him once your eyes are open to recognize Him present in the breaking of the bread. Have you ever reflected on the fact that a normal piece of bread was left broken on the table? This is as if to say, "Here I am; keep doing what I commanded and instructed." This is the means by which the transformation

---

[66] We must not only begin with Moses, we also need to start with the Genesis of our own lives. He has always been there walking alongside us, hidden behind the perplexities and contradictions of our past stories, in the same way that He is working through all the misfortunes and tragedies recorded in the Old Testament scriptures in all of human history.

of the world will be manifested in your midst. Eyes will continue to be opened in this sacrament.

> *"Then the two from Emmaus told their story of how Jesus had appeared to them as they were walking along the road, and how they had recognized him as he was breaking the bread." (Luke 24:35 NLT)*

## From The Mountain to the Table

The transfiguration means things can be glorious while still appearing common. The glory the disciples saw on the mountain was always in Him, just not accessible to their senses. At Emmaus, Jesus takes upon the form of the ordinary world, acting as a stranger. This is as if to say, "I am everywhere, moving behind the things that appear normal and mundane." Nothing is what it seems until you filter all things through the Word to see how all of history, including the story of your life, reveals Jesus. Each of us individually, along with all of humanity, are traveling on this same Emmaus road wrestling with life's perplexities. We are like those disciples, journeying with false expectations and disappointments. Often blinded by frustrations and pain, we cannot see how any of this world makes sense to us. The disciples said; "We hoped he was the one that was going to redeem Israel." Of course, he did not redeem only Israel, but the entire world—just not in the way any of them expected. Being constantly challenged to adjust our perspective to obtain a clear vision of God's dealings with us, and the world around us, is exhausting. The glorified Lord, the same one who was transfigured on the mountain, comes to us in a strange form again, this time admonishing us to change the way we see the world, because the world as we know it has already been changed in his very person. After what was accomplished in the transformation of all creation in His glorified body, he doesn't need to prove Himself anymore. The fact that He can come in normal form like the bread and the wine, and the world can remain unchanged, is more impressive than his transfiguration. What we need is a paradigm shift in our perspective to see the new creation working behind all things, especially in the transfigured elements.

## Dining with Jesus at His Kingdom

A very powerful image comes to mind when thinking about the broken bread administered by the resurrected Christ Himself. He disappeared before their eyes, but in reality He is now more clear than he's ever been; they realized He has already transformed the world, and the elements are left on the table to serve as a witness that He is dining with them at His kingdom table. Once we connect the transfiguration with the communion, the words of Christ become more relevant when He said:

> *"Jesus said, 'I have been very eager to eat this Passover meal with you before my suffering begins. For I tell you now that I won't eat this meal again until its meaning is fulfilled in the Kingdom of God. For I will not drink wine again until the Kingdom of God has come.'" (Luke 22:15-16, 18 NLT)*

When I used to read these verses, my presupposition was that one day we would partake of the Lord's Supper in heaven. The double annunciation of these statements, plus the context of the transfiguration previously discussed, seemed to point to the possibility that the hidden allusion of this passage is to the fulfillment of Passover in Jesus' death and resurrection[67]. This means that the Passover meal itself will be transformed into a new ritual, which will enable the Lord Himself to partake with His disciples of communion in a new intimate and transformative way in the Kingdom of God.[68]

---

[67] This Passover is special and different because of its relationship to Jesus' sufferings on the cross. After that moment, the meal will never be the same again, for it will reach consummation in the Kingdom of God.

[68] Study of the word fulfilled.

The disciples now know because of the transfiguration that it is possible to access a realm where the higher you spiritually climb, the farther you can naturally reach to restore the sufferings, pains, and brokenness of the world. As a result of Jesus' sacrifice, all the pain of creation was laid upon Him, so that now by His stripes we are healed. The Lord's Supper is the meeting place between heaven and Earth, the new realm where the reality of God's future is celebrated in our present. *The new creation will be in the presence of God: the expansion, extension, and redefinition of our daily existence.* We are practicing and developing that new Kingdom culture whenever we commune together with the Lord by partaking of His glorified body and drinking of the new covenant cup.

> *"And just as my Father has granted me a Kingdom, I now grant you the right to eat and drink at my table in my Kingdom." (Luke 22:29-30 NLT)*

> *"Look! I stand at the door and knock. If you hear my voice and open the door, I will come in, and we will share a meal together as friends. Those who are victorious will sit with me on my throne, just as I was victorious and sat with my Father on his throne." (Revelation 3:20-21 NLT)*

## Communion, The Eternalized Life

One may wonder: how exactly does eating and drinking prepare the heart for the world to come? In what way is the transformation of all things present, or even relevant, at the moment we partake of the rite of holy communion? When partaking of the Eucharist, the nature of Jesus and the revelation of His sacrifice informs our decisions and way of thinking in this life; then we begin to invest ourselves in heaven, establishing divine foundations of character that God uses to build His new creation. When we take communion, those strong convictions and values that are cemented in who we are as human beings have eternal weight to God, and he preserves them to shape the future He is creating for us in Glory. *In the sacrament of worship, we need to be filled with* the fullness of God, because just as in the present time the body contains the soul, so will the soul sustain the transformed universe in the age to come. Think about certain ways we eternalize our lives through the rite of the Lord's Supper.

1. *The relationships we encounter at the Lord's table are preordained to be cultivated and established, now and forever.* It is interesting to point out that the life Jesus shared with his disciples was honored at the Last Supper, elevated to an immortal status. The twelve belong to the lamb, now and forever. Those who found meaning and fulfillment in his company are permanently eternalized as part of His illustrious inner circle.

> *"You have stayed with me in my time of trial. And just as my Father has granted me a Kingdom, I now grant you the right to eat and drink at my table in my Kingdom. And you will sit on thrones, judging the twelve tribes of Israel." (Luke 22:28–30 NLT)*

> *"Jesus replied, 'I assure you that when the world is made new and the Son of Man sits upon his glorious throne, you who have been my followers will also sit on twelve thrones, judging the twelve tribes of Israel.'" (Matthew 19:28 NLT)*

> *"The wall of the city had twelve foundation stones, and on them were written the names of the twelve apostles of the Lamb." (Revelation 21:14 NLT)*

For our current study, we should absorb this challenge with sincerity and faith. In what way are we allowing the rite of communion to adequately esteem the relationships we share today to prepare us for God's eternal purposes? The scriptures clearly state that God has appointed the time, place, and genealogy of all the peoples in our world.

"From one man he created all the nations throughout the whole earth. He decided beforehand when they should rise and fall, and he determined their boundaries." (Acts of the Apostles 17:26 NLT)

That means there are no coincidences or accidents in regards to eternal matters on the earth. We are supposed to celebrate each other, and discover the hidden treasures inside one another for delight, fulfillment, and glory. *Our spiritual connections are echoes of the voice of purpose emanating from God's memories.* Jesus explained that when someone is immersed in the experience of living in the Kingdom, God Himself filters all interactions through those around them.

> *"And this is the will of God, that I should not lose even one of all those he has given me, but that I should raise them up at the last day. For no one can come to me unless the Father who sent me draws them to me, and at the last day I will raise them up. As it is written in the Scriptures, 'They will all be taught by God.' Everyone who listens to the Father and learns from him comes to me." (John 6:39, 44-45 NLT)*

We have to trust that God would not allow anyone to get close to us unless there was a divine transaction from the world to come that needed to be addressed in the present. How is it that some people can come in and out of our lives, and they're always welcome in the same manner as though they never left? On the other hand, there are some acquaintances that, no matter how hard you try, you can never get them to be a part of who you are. I believe our steps have been ordered to follow an established path in regards to partnerships and relationships in the Kingdom—just like in a wedding, in which you desire to be surrounded by special people who are significant to that momentous event. In the same manner, it should be meaningful who we break the bread of the Kingdom with when we celebrate God's royal meal. It is a way of saying to God; we are assimilating what you have predestined. Communion is declaring; "Lord, your Kingdom is coming and is already inaugurated in our hearts. We are living in the meaningful company of people that together have immortalized God's covenant faithfulness to our lives." What will God have for you to do in the new heavens and the new earth? Only the things that pertain to the faith, hope, and love that you are practicing with those he has placed around you. According to 1 Corinthians 13, everything else will cease; only those specific virtues will remain. In 1 Corinthians 6, Paul seems to address this very issue when he suggests that our ongoing social predicaments are testing us to reveal the true capacity of our future eternal stature.

> *"When one of you has a dispute with another believer, how dare you file a lawsuit and ask a secular court to decide the matter instead of taking it to other believers! Don't you realize that someday we believers will judge the world? And since you are going to judge the world, can't you decide even these little things among yourselves? Don't you realize that we will judge angels? So you should surely be able to resolve ordinary disputes in this life." (1 Corinthians 6:1-3 NLT)*

No one likes conflicts, but these trials are essential to verify the fruit of our Christlikeness. What unites us at the table should be stronger than what separates us from it. If not, we are failing the divine tests and jeopardizing our eternal inheritance. Notice this interesting perspective Paul uses to address the abuses of the Lord's table.

> *"But, of course, there must be divisions among you so that you who have God's approval will be recognized!" (1 Corinthians 11:19 NLT)*

*2. The consequences of sin, and its debilitating effects on our conscience, can be decisively mended and resolved to freely live for God's future.* I believe there is a tremendous weight of guilt that we constantly suppress deep within our consciences. The consequences of our iniquities torment us, carrying unspoken shame and discontent. This residue of regret and remorse is unbearable to our souls. Words we should have said that were left unspoken. Hurtful comments and damaging conversations that we wish we had avoided. Events that marred our self-esteem and forever traumatized our memory, constantly reminding us of past failures. What hope is there for us who desire to one day stand before God to bring a life worthy of His praise? One of the ways I believe communion prepares us for God's future is by restoring our perception of the record of our past life. In other words, God cleanses our conscience, setting us free from our history so it cannot affect us anymore in what pertains to our future. Now we can freely live for Him, behaving as though we have never sinned. Our dignity is restored, so that we can have boldness and confidence to minister to others on his behalf. This is not just a comforting thought. This is at the core and center of the purpose of the Lord's table.

> *"As he spoke, he showed them the wounds in his hands and his side. They were filled with joy when they saw the Lord! Again he said, 'Peace be with you. As the Father has sent me, so I am sending you.' Then he breathed on them and said, 'Receive the Holy Spirit. If you forgive anyone's sins, they are forgiven. If you do not forgive them, they are not forgiven.'" (John 20:20-23 NLT)*

This commissioning is important, because it shows how the effects of our fallen nature have been dealt with on the body of the resurrected Son of God. Death itself has been defeated. Everything destructive, decaying, corrupted, and temporal has been transformed in the Lord's glorified body. Jesus is standing before the disciples, and He is breathing new creation into them. He is saying that what Adam lost in the unfinished project of creation is still on course towards God's allotted destiny. The main characteristic of this miraculous work accomplished in Jesus' broken body is the peculiar and divine ability to forgive sins. Notice how from now on, forgiven people with the breath of new creation can restore and transform all things that were fallen and decaying through the power of forgiveness. This delegated grace communicated by the risen Lord is practiced every time the Eucharist is celebrated. The broken body of Christ was given so that in the power of the Spirit, all things that are currently dying can become alive again with the hope for a new future in the new creation. Think about the example of the apostle Paul. How can anyone with such a horrible past be consecrated as the primary caretaker of the very communities he persecuted and decimated?

> *"This is a trustworthy saying, and everyone should accept it: 'Christ Jesus came into the world to save sinners'—and I am the worst of them all. But God had mercy on me so that Christ Jesus could use me as a prime example of his great patience with even the worst sinners. Then others will realize that they, too, can believe in him and receive eternal life." (1 Timothy 1:15-16 NLT)*

How would you behave, talk, think, and live if your entire record in life would be wiped clean? This is the power of the Lord's table in practical application. We come to start afresh, to truly live for the glory of God.

*3. The discipline of surrendering our lives, sacrificing them in a Christlike manner.* This is one feature of our eternal worship that we practice and perfect at the communion table. The amazement of the wonder of the cross is revisited in humility at communion. Contemplating the eternal price that was paid for our salvation reminds us of the true value of all the things we have received as sacred. This is important to cultivate in our hearts, a culture of honor in progression towards the majesty of God. To advance forward into deeper realms of God's glory, we must learn the heavenly ethics of consecration and sanctification. That means mastering the art of letting go of inferior things, recognizing greater worth in what we assimilate in the partaking of the elements. When the blood purchased all things in redemption, it set an incalculable value on the dignity of our spiritual devotion to God. This could be a difficult argument to make, but meditate with me on how celebrating the blood and broken body of Jesus' sacrifice is like reliving the auctioning of things that, at one time, were perceived as lost, insignificant, and forgotten. But now these items have been raised in stock because of the desirability they obtained from their purchaser.

*"For you know that God paid a ransom to save you from the empty life you inherited from your ancestors. And it was not paid with mere gold or silver, which lose their value. It was the precious blood of Christ, the sinless, spotless Lamb of God. God chose him as your ransom long before the world began, but now in these last days he has been revealed for your sake." (1 Peter 1:18–20 NLT)*

How real will we allow that transaction to be in our souls, regulating our affections and governing the administration of our lives? I believe this exercise of evaluation celebrated in the Eucharist prepares us in the present for the handling of eternal matters in the world to come. Here we are, contemplating one of the most vital components of the transformation of the heart, when handling the cup of our salvation. Every time we partake of the cup and bread of the Kingdom, we are acknowledging the true significance of all things eternal in relation to God. This helps us to change our perception of our earthly existence, and adjust our spiritual lenses to see things through God's eyes. We acquire a new set of values, investing more fully into God's future. The Lord's Supper gives us the ability to not devalue the precious, or become overfamiliar with the divine. The Eucharist is training us in the art of finding transcendent attributes in all things sacred, admiring what they represent in their essence and not being distracted by their appearances.

## The Cup of Judgement

The unthinkable happened in Jesus' life and ministry, in that He as a high priest sat upon the throne of God.

*"Now of the things which we have spoken this is the sum: We have such a high priest, who is set on the right hand of the throne of the Majesty in the heavens; a minister of the sanctuary, and of the true tabernacle, which the Lord pitched, and not man." (Hebrews 8:1–2 KJV)*

Who would have imagined that a high priest could take such a prominent position? The ark of the covenant was the symbol of the throne of God on Earth; there was the glory seated upon the cherubim, as it was seen in the visions of the prophets and the psalms of scripture. Jesus is in the heavens interceding for us right now, making the throne of justice and judgment also the place of mercy and forgiveness (Heb 4:14-16). He is also, by the power of the Spirit, letting us know what He receives and shares in the glory of our Father. Here on Earth, the gifts of the Spirit, the forgiveness of sins, the experience of worship, the communion of prayer, and the grace of service and instruction all serve as evidence of His effective ministry, showing the authority of His dominion from the heavens to bring the kingdom of God to Earth. Where can we experience all this wonderful display of Jesus' glorious ministry? That's what the Church is all about—the body of Christ, the corporal reality of God on Earth, where we experience God through others and God also experiences others through us; where joy, peace, and righteousness are perfected and hope, faith, and love are practiced and established among the saints. No wonder Hebrews concludes by declaring: "Let us hold fast the confession of our hope without wavering, not forsaking our own assembling together, as is the habit of some" (Heb 10:23-25). Let's therefore encourage one another all the more now that we see that the day is drawing near.

The high priests enter in the day of atonement to the holy of holies, in a solemn day of resolution and consummation. So it is every time we approach the high priest of our faith, who offers the bread and wine of the new covenant before the Father. It is a moment of judgment, in which the king on the throne will rule in our favor because of the excellence of his priestly office. What an amazing privilege, to visit the throne of glory in advance to resolve our traumas and inner conflicts, knowing beforehand that our conscience has been cleansed of all guilt and shame. In many ways, the day of atonement was the medium by which God addressed the condition of the temple, the people, and the land. In order to continue offering worship acceptable to God, the iniquities and the defilement of things holy needed to be confronted. In this day, the priesthood representing the people ensured that the continual influence of the presence of God would remain active in the land. One of the ways to understand the celebration of the Eucharist is the exercise of the rededication of our faith. When we celebrate it, we ensure that we are continuing in the Lord's original vision of love and consecration for his will. The many things that lurk hidden, or are unknown to our minds, are addressed in order not to hinder the grace that rests upon our lives. In order to see more of God working through us as his chosen vessels, we need to have this prototype day of judgment administrated in us by communion.

> *"So anyone who eats this bread or drinks this cup of the Lord unworthily is guilty of sinning against the body and blood of the Lord. That is why you should examine yourself before eating the bread and drinking the cup. For if you eat the bread or drink the cup without honoring the body of Christ, you are eating and drinking God's judgment upon yourself." (1 Corinthians 11:27-29 NLT)*

The language of judgment brings to mind the image of the throne of God. That is the place where heavenly transactions are made, and the word of the king is proclaimed to be executed as his divine commandment. In the old covenant, that throne of authority was not only mirrored in the holy of holies, it was actually manifested when the glory sat in the midst of the cherubim. When Paul speaks of judgment, he describes the scenes of God's Heavenly courtroom. That throne of kingship is now active on Earth in a special way through Jesus, our heavenly high priest. We are emulating on Earth the ascension of our king, who presented before the Father his body and blood before the throne, in the consecration of the bread and wine. We are joining the glory, honor, and power that were given to the son of man before the ancient days. This is a way of us saying to the Lord, "Take dominion and execute your judgments, starting with us your people, who believe and are seated in heavenly places at your kingdom table." This is why we should approach the sacraments with holy introspection, examining ourselves so that the kingdom of God can saturate our souls.

Often, people wonder how they ought to live their lives now that they belong to the family of God. How is their redemption or salvation affected by their sinful behavior? I believe some of these issues are indirectly addressed in Paul's treatment of the abuses of the Lord's table. When the Corinthians distorted the Lord's communion, Paul was forced to explain the meaning and significance of this rite at the center of Christian life. A few things come to mind in realizing this conclusion; notice that there is a difference between judgment to the people of God and to the people outside the covenant (1 Corinthians 11:32). Most importantly, this distinction is a sacramental differentiation. In other words, this separation between God's dealing with his people, and His interactions with those outside the covenant, is supposed to be upheld and celebrated at the Lord's table. For those who are inside the family of God, there is only one true focus with which we should concern our lives: not to sin against the body and blood of our Lord. Because we are his temple, whatever we do with our bodies, we are in reality doing to His own possession. Now that we are the body of the messiah, whatever we do to Christ's members is offensive to him. We would be dishonoring His sacrifice and ignoring the value and purpose of his blood if we didn't allow his divine life to find expression through our lives, especially in our interactions and relationships with others. That is why it is so important to belong to a fellowship table, where we can experience and celebrate this heavenly transaction of self-examination.

The Christian life is a continual pursuit of alignment with the depth of meaning of the life, death, and resurrection of our Lord Jesus Christ. To become an extension of his vision, embodying his heart and mission, we need this special communion table at the center of our devotions. This is an amazing benefit for believers, allowing us to prepare ourselves for final judgment with preliminary hearings in the presence of God. We need the Judge to rule over our lives in our favor for the clearing of our conscience and to fulfill his purposes. If there are truths that we are proclaiming in theory, but not applying in practice, we need to reflect on these inconsistencies as we partake of this internal judgment to protect ourselves from all hypocrisy and self-deception. Every doctrine, dogma, and teaching that is not absorbed in the Lord's communion is potentially an error that is disguised as an appealing truth. Such erroneous convictions need to be examined and investigated; we must dissect them under the auspices of the cross. That way, we can guard against all spiritual strongholds that could make our hearts insensitive to the true purposes of God. One of the main issues with educated believers is that they may figure out ways to manipulate truth to suit their own conveniences. Hidden motives and secret agendas go unchecked, lurking behind the proclamation of half-truths that don't lead to the unity, sanctification, and honoring of the Lord's body. The time of examining ourselves in communion gives our hearts an opportunity to reflect on all our internal conflicts and polluted intentions that need to be confronted and transformed. At the end of the day, what good can come from truths that we boldly proclaim but in reality don't enjoy? The Lord's Supper gives us an opportunity to live out the joy of our Christianity. That way, we finally get an encounter with reality, to find realization and understanding of the full meaning of our salvation.

Standing at the administration of the elements, one would be face to face with the reality of Jesus' redemptive work. That is a good moment to ask ourselves self-examining questions:

- What does Jesus' death mean to me, and in what way am I living today by his example?

- If Jesus' vision is his table, in what way am I allowing those who surround my life to be a part of my spiritual family, and to be with the Lord at the table for them?

- How am I promoting the sacramental life, causing everyone around me to acknowledge that I am truly in covenant and prioritizing the fellowship table of the Lord?

*"Wherefore whosoever shall eat this bread, and drink this cup of the Lord unworthily shall be guilty of the body and blood of the Lord." (1 Corinthians 11:27 KJV)*

Why not guilty of eating incorrectly, or losing sight of the spiritual significance of the sacraments? Is this statement supposed to imply that we are guilty over what happened on the cross if we mishandle the table? If what happened on the cross was for my redemption, how can I be guilty of it? Perhaps this phrase goes beyond the immediate context of simply mishandling the elements of the Lord's Supper. If the table is understood correctly as the equivalent of the Lord Himself and His redemptive work, then to abuse its purpose opens the conversation to much larger implications. Maybe now that our entire beings are absorbed into membership in the Lord's body, we are viewed in light of the specific fellowship table to which we belong, examining carefully the condition of our entire sacramental life. This is a profound statement, for it will signify that at either side of the cross, there is judgment—both for those outside the covenant who have not allowed the sacrifice of the cross to change their lives, and then for those inside the covenant who are misunderstanding or abusing the purpose of the Lord's death.

> *"For he that eateth and drinketh unworthily, eateth and drinketh damnation to himself, not discerning the Lord's body." (1 Corinthians 11:29 KJV)*

It is interesting that while reflecting on the chastisement of the Lord, Paul interprets this judgment as positive. Anything that keeps us within the confines of the household of faith is viewed in a good light. We are the benefactors of a great salvation, the recipients of an incredible grace. Nevertheless, we are not to make light of these gifts and graces that are conferred upon us. When Paul is thinking about these issues, he reflects on the children of Israel in the desert:

> *"I don't want you to forget, dear brothers and sisters, about our ancestors in the wilderness long ago. All of them were guided by a cloud that moved ahead of them, and all of them walked through the sea on dry ground. In the cloud and in the sea, all of them were baptized as followers of Moses, and all of them drank the*

*same spiritual water. For they drank from the spiritual rock that traveled with them, and that rock was Christ. Yet God was not pleased with most of them, and their bodies were scattered in the wilderness." (1 Corinthians 10:1-2, 4-5 NLT)*

Being rescued and delivered is not the end of the story. Having escaped as the chosen people of God introduces us to a new responsibility: how are we going to manage and handle this salvation that was given to us? The Lord's Supper is one of the places where we manage our responsibilities in a very specific and precise way.

# 5

# The Figurative Language of the Lord's Supper

*Dining with Parables and Symbols*

The communities of believers that celebrated the Lord's Supper practiced their ritual in the format of a full dinner within the tradition of a Greco-Roman banquet. Jesus' Passover meal, and most retellings of the Gospels' stories of reunions, follow this same standard model of first-century hospitality. When the church was reading of Jesus' dinner celebrations, that was of particular importance to them. This information offered significant theological resources that illuminated their minds on how to conduct themselves at their own fellowship meetings. More significantly, Jesus' formalities and etiquette situated their rituals within the perspective of the Kingdom of God, which they sought to apprehend during their worship gatherings. In the Gospels, Jesus was invited as a guest of honor to dinner tables and often served by suspicious and reluctant hosts. He was treated unceremoniously on different occasions by those invited to the banquet, yet also surprisingly appreciated by unusual, unexpected guests. All this material offers a rich pool of insight for the communities of believers that were eager to derive principles to instruct and shape their own respective ceremonial meals. Whether private or public, all dinner celebrations where Jesus was present had one thing in common; there were always parables taught to illustrate the Kingdom of God. It seems that in the Gospel narratives, allegories shared at dinner give the audience the best opportunity to confront relational issues, discuss doctrinal conflicts, and challenge well-established social conventions. The evangelists present Jesus illuminating different, difficult scenarios through stories at dinner reunions, expressing answers in the Kingdom of God that had already been already inaugurated in His person. As churches were gathering around a meal, and they had been presented with the story of Jesus partaking of dinners and telling stories about a kingdom that was consummated in a banquet, the importance of these parables in relation to the Lords' Supper becomes significantly clearer. Whether it be the controversial dining with Levi the tax collector, or the scandalous encounter with the sinner woman who poured oil at Jesus' feet, or even the man who was healed of dropsy in the Pharisees' house, every occasion of the breaking of bread had a counter-perspective view that needed unveiling through the Kingdom's lens of Jesus' majestic parables. It is almost as if the Lord was inviting people to see a different realm through communion, just beneath the surface of their everyday affairs. One can argue that Jesus' meals were themselves parabolic in nature, like an invitation to His symbolic, otherworldly manner of viewing reality. The way he enacted scriptures, subverted common expectations at dinner parties, and interpreted spiritual significances in the actions and responses to Him at the table were all ways of depicting fellowship with Him as a sacred, symbolic activity.

In other words, we can see that behind some of the retellings of Jesus' house visits, there are indirect instructions on how to handle Jesus' sacramental presence. We are seeing firsthand that one of the most important lessons to learned when hosting the Lord at our fellowship reunions is how to think symbolically. We need the transformation of our imagination to see ourselves as part of the characters inside the divine drama of the Lord's Supper. The Bible's parables of Jesus are like our script, and the theater of our lives is the canopy where God's novel will be fully revealed when we partake of holy communion. What are some examples of these Biblical protocols that we can adopt to imaginatively assume a role at Jesus' Kingdom Banquet? Luke tells us some insightful instructions as a Pharisee invited Jesus to recline with him at the table.

"Then he turned to the woman and said to Simon, 'Look at this woman kneeling here. When I entered your home, you didn't offer me water to wash the dust from my feet, but she has washed them with her tears and wiped them with her hair. You didn't greet me with a kiss, but from the time I first came in, she has not stopped kissing my feet. You neglected the courtesy of olive oil to anoint my head, but she has anointed my feet with rare perfume. I tell you, her sins—and they are many—have been forgiven, so she has shown me much love. But a person who is forgiven little shows only little love.' Then Jesus said to the woman, 'Your sins are forgiven'" (Luke 7:44-48 NLT).

*"And Jesus said to the woman, 'Your faith has saved you; go in peace.'" (Luke 7:50 NLT)*

Here we can see that with the renewing of our minds, there is forgiveness, redemption, and salvation accessible in the presence of Jesus when he is received as an honored guest at our fellowship table. If the Lord is properly appreciated and valued for who He really is in our lives, we can expect to see His affection, mercy, and compassion extended even to the worst of sinners. Our Lord is passionate towards us, broken and poured out in the elements of bread and wine, which illustrate complete abandonment to God's love. Indifference or carelessness to His sacramental presence is offensive to the ritual of communion. There is no room for apathy in the celebration of the greatest demonstration of passion the world has ever known. Jesus contrasts and makes a direct comparison between the Pharisee and the woman; even when she might not have a clue to what she's doing, her passion has exposed everything the religious leader has not done. A lot of what takes place at the breaking and drinking of the elements is similar to the dramatization of spiritual role-playing. We are challenged to embrace an emotional posture, engaging with defined plots and scripted lines in a story in which we participate. Are we like that Judas that betrayed the Lord at Passover, or a type of Peter who resisted the idea of the cross? Is our heart sensitive and receptive, like John resting upon the Lord's chest, hearing his most intimate thoughts and insights, or are we like the disciples who argued over the status and position of who would sit where at the table instead of paying attention to the Lord? This woman was hitting all the right notes, while the prominent religious leader was missing the whole point of communion. Such a dramatic scene; Jesus turned his back to his host, speaking to him while addressing his attention towards the woman. There is a contrast being drawn between the woman and the Pharisee. Everything she has done that was perceived as out of place actually exposed everything missing at that banquet.

In another story, Jesus challenged the guests at the house of Levi to imagine His disciples as the sons of the bridal chamber, and Himself as the bridegroom. By this parabolic vision of the events taking place in the festivities at Levi's house, Jesus interpreted, ate, and drank with His disciples as an expression of God's eschatological wedding banquet. To apply this perspective to the sacrament of the Eucharist will mean that the communities of believers reading these stories must handle Jesus' relationship with the church as an active, divine romance that needs careful administration. In John 3:29, a similar analogy is used: John the Baptist describing himself as the friend of the bridegroom, a title corresponding to the person who functions as the coordinator of a Jewish wedding. This designation was delegated to the person who handled the invitations to the celebration, and also played the master of ceremonies at the event. Most importantly, this loyal friend served as the trusted assistant to the bridegroom, the personal protector of his bride. This image was very helpful for churches who desired to conduct the Lord's Supper in a reverential manner. To think of the symposium portion of the Lord's Supper as an opportunity to convey prophetic love letters to the bride transformed the meeting of believers into a deeply moving occasion. Giving room for the Spirit to express heartfelt love songs to the bridegroom changed the way people prepared and received the formalities of their worship experience.

We can see how every one of these stories Jesus articulated had the incredible descriptive power to awaken the hearts of the communities away from the mundane, empty exercises of the pagan religions of their day. They could experience firsthand in the Kingdom meal a new and living way to be connected to God through the passages of the scriptures. The same should be true of us when we accept our roles within God's story. These texts are not just historical accounts to be observed at a safe distance. The passages describing the Lord's visitation at these dinner events all had miracles, healings, forgiveness, salvation, and restorations to open our minds to everything that is available to us when we encounter Jesus as our honored guest. We must become appreciative, like that debtor who was forgiven an unpayable debt, or grateful, like those guests who could not afford a place at the prestigious dinner banquet. We must be careful not to be like the host who simply followed the normal social conventions of the religious status quo. Our challenge in general is to assimilate the stories and parables of scripture, and see ourselves as part of the eternal drama that is unfolding at our worship gatherings. *The mind void of scriptural knowledge becomes a soul empty of divine inspiration. We must give the Holy Spirit something to work with.*

## The Table, the Temple, and the Homeland

When Jesus uses detailed descriptions in his stories, it is almost as if he were describing things very vivid and personal to Him. He is granting us access into his private psyche, persuading us to free our feelings and yield to the longings of our deepest dreams. Parables are like windows into Jesus' humanity, an entrance to his realm of intimacy with God. In order to address the hidden, unseen realm of the human heart and expose the innermost secrets that hinder our experience of the divine, the Lord relies on graphic and masterful storytelling.

Perhaps the most important and insightful story of them all is one we don't immediately connect as relevant when dealing with the Last Supper. There are several hints that one of Jesus' main images and figurative conceptions about the suffering of His body was the belief that, through His death, he was building a dwelling place for humanity and an eternal habitation for His father. We are talking about the parabolic language Jesus used about the temple, when He elucidated it in terms of being His Father's house.

*"Then, going over to the people who sold doves, he told them, 'Get these things out of here. Stop turning my Father's house into a marketplace!' Then his disciples remembered this prophecy from the Scriptures: 'Passion for God's house will consume me.'" (John 2:16-17 NLT)*

*"His parents didn't know what to think. 'Son,' his mother said to him, 'why have you done this to us? Your father and I have been frantic, searching for you everywhere.' 'But why did you need to search?' he asked. 'Didn't you know that I must be in my Father's house?'" (Luke 2:48-49 NLT)*

One of the most loveliest themes in the theology of Jesus is His conception of dwelling with the Father in an inseparable, eternal union. The portrait painted by Christ at the breaking of the bread is that, as part of His glorified body, we also have access to the dwelling of the Father by His Spirit. Seeing ourselves as sanctuaries or dwelling rooms in a mansion is not an easy idea to grasp; that is why Jesus taught us at His kingdom banquet to think symbolically. He is training us through His parables to sanctify our minds internally, and creatively visualize all the thoughts and images that represent peace and tranquility to us. Jesus instructed us at His kingdom meal to embrace His inspiration, and accept the total stability and protection of His sacramental presence. As a result of His sacrifice, we are supposed to finally be forever at home, secured at the Father's house to become transformed into His glorious temple. That is why at John's account of the Passover meal with the disciples, Jesus said:

*"Don't let your hearts be troubled. Trust in God, and trust also in me. There is more than enough room in my Father's home. If this were not so, would I have told you that I am going to prepare a place for you? When everything is ready, I will come and get you, so that you will always be with me where I am. And you know the way to where I am going."*

*"I am the way, the truth, and the life. No one can come to the Father except through me." (John 14:1-4, 6 NLT)*

Jesus is clearly elucidating the meaning of His broken body in relation to the reconstitution of God's house. The cleansing at the temple that Jesus describes as His Father's house pointed to the eschatological event of a new dwelling place for God being reconstructed in His glorified body. That is why Jesus said, "Destroy this temple and in three days I will rebuild it," and John clarified that he was talking about his own body. Here we have yet another prophetic picture to better understand the administration of Jesus' symbolic actions at the Passover meal. When we partake of the body and blood of the Messiah, we are literally feasting at the Father's house, preparing ourselves for the glory of progressively becoming His temple.

*"Consequently, you are no longer foreigners and strangers, but fellow citizens with God's people and also members of his household, built on the foundation of the apostles and prophets, with Christ Jesus himself as the chief cornerstone. In him the whole building is joined together and rises to become a holy temple in the Lord. And in him you too are being built together to become a dwelling in which God lives by his Spirit." (Ephesians 2:19-22)*

In the Bible, the human condition is that of a restless soul without a habitat to truly flourish spiritually. Expelled from the garden, wandering in the desert, exiled from the promised land, and ultimately removed from God's presence, the story of the scriptures is that of a people without a home. Not only humanity, but God Himself shares this experience because of man's fall. He was left without the temple that would serve as the permanent resting place for His manifestation. God's dream always was for us to become His house, and the eternal dwelling of His glorious image. But because of our sin, we have alienated God from enjoying communion and intimacy with His creation, and have not allowed the full disclosure and revelation of everything He is and has for us.

Now Jesus, the Creator that was separated from His creation, and humanity, which was alienated from God, can both find a new sanctuary to dwell together forever in unity and love. The scripture says the Word became flesh because divinity and humanity were wrapped in one bodily form. The Church is called the body of Christ because we, as the people of God, were never meant to be a place that is visited, but a family you join to become the new living tabernacle of God's glory. The desire of our Heavenly Father is that we develop a strong sense of belonging, feasting at His kingdom. That we appropriated His blood results in an atmosphere of acceptance, which inspires delight and trust. His divine nature is shared with us in the elements of communion, which heal our wounds, restore our souls, and embrace the fulfillment and satisfaction of being at home in His presence. We need to stop seeing ourselves as orphans, because the Holy Spirit has been sent to our hearts to make our union with Christ's table a clear revelation of the love of our Father.

> *"No, I will not abandon you as orphans—I will come to you. When I am raised to life again, you will know that I am in my Father, and you are in me, and I am in you."*
>
> *"All who love me will do what I say. My Father will love them, and we will come and make our home with each of them." (John 14:18, 20, 23 NLT)*

When we gather together to celebrate the Eucharist, we ought to think as a family that is inseparably linked together to host the presence of God. There is healing for all the broken and missing pieces of our humanity when we internalize the idea that we were made to be inhabited by God's glory, consumed by His irresistible love and reflecting eternally His righteous image. When Jesus says he won't leave us as orphans at the Last Supper, that carries significant weight for our wounded hearts. This statement signifies that our internal condition, without the supervision of the divine nature of God, is like an abandoned, hopeless child that is left alone to perish. Away from the Father's house, we are traumatized and damaged souls, confused emotionally and deformed spiritually. This is a very compelling characterization of our personal experience of emptiness without God! In the absence of union with Christ, our social abnormalities and personality distortions will sabotage our destiny. Imagine growing without being celebrated or embraced, surviving while lacking emotional support or personal understanding. Eventually, one will never seek or care to be understood, affirmed, or known by others. Accountability will be avoided, connectedness will be seen as repugnant, and introversion or isolation will become the preferred course of action above anything else in life. In a time when one out of three children died by the age of ten because of abandonment, and kids without parents were cruelly viewed as the equivalent of dogs, Jesus' use of the word "orphan" was very striking. He is describing the predominant state of humanity without intimacy with God in the most alarming way possible. This, in light of our textual analysis about parables and symbols, gives us colorful pictures to inform our understanding of what a relationship with Christ is supposed to stimulate in us. In the gospel of John, the model of Jesus as God's residence is subtly placed at the start of the book's narrative, introducing Him to Nathanael as the one to whom all scriptures and prophets point. Jesus then interprets His own work and ministry to all who have eyes to perceive by saying:

> *"Then he said, 'I tell you the truth, you will all see heaven open and the angels of God going up and down on the Son of Man, the one who is the stairway between heaven and earth.'" (John 1:51 NLT)*

Everything that follows is being elucidated by the Lord Himself as the heavenly activity of God's new Bethel, the Old Testament name used to describe God's house. All the signs of the miracles of Jesus are happening on Earth, because God's residence is finally available to mankind.

## Dining at the Father's House

We have already illuminated the parables of Jesus as spiritual devices to apprehend His symbolic world at God's banquet. Let's now immerse ourselves in the most detailed and graphic banquet story of them all. We are referring to the famous parable of the prodigal son. Historically, this story has some interesting undertones that can bring out some key elements of our study. During the first century, Israel as God's nation was fragmented, having difficulty conserving and establishing its true identity. Many Jews, even when back at their homeland, were still compromised spiritually and politically, while others spread throughout the nations were facing challenges to maintain their ancestry. Socially and culturally, many of God's chosen people were losing their Jewish heritage. Jesus presented a new solution with his parables, a radical alternative to the nation's internal struggles. Introducing Himself as the new temple of God, Jesus was proposing a total transformation and redefinition of the nation's identity around his person. In Him, the hopeless lost sheep of the house of Israel could be returned to the fold. Like the story of the lost coin, the incalculable value of the image of God in each person can be recovered back to the remaining whole. Prodigal sons wandering in foreign lands can find their way back home, and elder brothers who have stayed at the homeland can rediscover the real meaning of belonging to the Father's house.

This would mean that Jesus sees stranded and exiled Israel in an immature stage, driven by confused impulses and victimized by circumstances out of its control, and as a result, totally out of touch with the true self of the nation. On the other hand, national Israel is depicted as an elder brother who is supposed to know better, yet in being more seasoned and experienced, he has become arrogant, cold, and insensitive to the Father and His vision of a new restored Israel revealed in the Son of God. The controversy surrounding Jesus' parables in Luke 15 revolved around the gatherings of all sorts of unusual people who were eating with Him. The parabolic answer is that in Jesus, the Father is restoring national Israel to finally be at home, feasting in the experience of the kingdom of God. Translating this anecdote to the context of a community table would have very powerful applications for the church. We are all either the lost, immature son without a home looking to blaze our own trail with the Father's inheritance, or the insensitive elder brother who, having all at our disposal, fails to see the true value of our place at the house with pure motives.

## The Younger Son

I find in the character of the prodigal son an illustration of the deep compulsion of the human heart to seek autonomy. To be truly our own masters, we strive with eagerness to prove to ourselves or others that we can make it on our own. In that mentality, we resist dependency on others, or the commitment to emotionally support those around us. The resentment in this tale can be felt when the young son basically says to his Father, "You are as good to me as dead, just give me what is mine!" When our perception of God only allows us to conceive of the things to which we feel we are entitled, our connectedness or sense of community will no longer have any importance to us. Then we become ready to quickly move on from anything or anyone that represents our heritage; because it is too humbling to live in gratitude, we prefer to starve in self-reliance and reject any remembrance of where we truly come from. The delusions of grandeur, and the ambition of seeking a life greater than the humanity God ordained for us to embrace, spark an attitude of defiance in which we just want out of any duty or personal obligation. It's time to be free from the burdens of loyalty and kinship and strive towards independence, totally detached from personal or meaningful associations.

The scripture says that the younger son gathered everything together and journeyed to a distant country. I believe the revelation of the Lord's table is for all those that are tired of journeying away, seeking for something that doesn't exist. People who have reached a turning point in their lives, and don't need or care to prove anything to anyone anymore.

We might not know exactly what fueled the young's son's insolence, but we are told he reached a place of remorse and regret. Perhaps he left with venom in his soul because of the conflicts with his brother, his animosity towards his father, or his general discontent with who he was in relation to others. Yet now he can't think of anything better than being close to the supervision and care of his father. Just being there at home is enough; his focus is totally in having rest for his soul, forgiveness, and the comfort of knowing that his father understands how sorry he is for what he has done. Many will never enjoy the full experience of the Lord's table until they can see themselves as prodigals returning home. What makes a home significant and meaningful are the relationships that are celebrated within it. The Lord's Supper represents a life of bonding and interdependence, in which we are celebrated for who we are and not for what we can do or what we possess. This parable paints a vivid picture, showing that when a real crisis comes, having a true home is the only thing that really matters.

## The Elder Brother

In many ways, this particular character could very well be the main focus of the parable. Undoubtedly he represents the immediate audience of Christ, which was grumbling about his banquet practices with sinners. It is interesting that the parable ends with the father pleading with his eldest son, as if the story is open-ended, waiting for the response of the hearers to decide how it will end. Similar to his brother, this son is filled with deep and complex issues of disenfranchisement; his heart is polluted and twisted, and the sad part is he doesn't even know it. This description of national Israel as the elder brother could be of particular interest to the church. If the leaders, scribes, and professional interpreters of the scriptures could not accept their own Messiah, what makes us think we are not in danger of making the same mistake they made and not recognizing the body of Christ? We could very well end up like this elder brother, always looking for greater levels of influence, prestige, and recognition, and totally missing the point of what it really means to belong to the Father. Some of us could end up being so infatuated with the Father's inheritance that all we see at the table is who has what, and all we think about is how we can get more of it than the others. Like national Israel, we may falsely assume that our calling is all about celebrating ourselves, and in our fascination with being elected, we may end up excluding others we were originally chosen to restore. Could it be that some at the church are working at the house to appear big in the sight of others, or even attempting to earn greater favor from the Father? Let's look at some of the interesting and overlooked details of this character in the story, which could help us understand Christ's lessons on how not to behave at the father's house.

*1. The elder brother is described as unable to control his emotions.* The Bible said he was angry, furious—so much so that he elected to make a scene, publicly dishonoring his father. In his protest of not entering the house, he made his father stop his hosting duties to go outside and plead with him. It was all about his feelings, and he wanted everyone to feel his pain; overtaken by bitterness, he was stealing the joy of his own father, who was enjoying the resurrection of his other son.

When our truth makes us lose sight of empathy, and our insights cause us to no longer be interested in understanding or relating to the condition of others, that self-righteousness is destructive to our humanity. We can become cold-hearted and insensitive, only able to absorb ourselves in things that concern our personal interest. The religious leaders of Jesus' day were so invested in their political status and moral superiority over common peasants that they no longer were able to experience compassion for the needy, or exercise mercy towards the fallen within their country. This elder brother speaks to us about our emotional condition, asking us the question: what is disturbing us, and why are we offended by the celebration of others? Are we at the house unable to celebrate our brothers and sisters because the party is not centered around us? Are we insinuating that if we are not the focus of attention, no one should be able to experience joy? The fellowship table of the Lord is not a feast for spoiled brats, it is a communal convocation for the acknowledgment of others in the unity and appreciation they share as members of the family. Emotional instability could be a sign of spiritual bankruptcy, especially when it affects our interactions with others who are a part of our life. The spirituality that does not produce self-control and cannot be lived in close proximity to others is a form of false piety. Out-of-control emotions are like a warning, alarming us that something has gone wrong in our hearts, especially when there is resentment and frustration in a place we are supposed to cherish kindness and benevolence.

*2. There is an allusion in the parable to an impersonal approach to seeking understanding.* The older son's superficial associations have replaced meaningful connections. If there were any questions, why not go straight to the source; in this case, the father? The best way to get a true sense of any situation is directly addressing the people that are involved in the matter. Even the servant hints at the fact that this brother should know better.

> *"Your brother is back,' he was told, 'and your father has killed the fattened calf. We are celebrating because of his safe return.'" (Luke 15:27 NLT)*

Notice the words the servant uses—your brother, your father, received him safe and sound—in contrast with the words the elder brother uses: your son, you have never given me, to make merry with my friends. This elder brother is detached from the sense of belonging, and his way of approaching circumstances is totally narcissistic. He views people as means to an end, not as meaningful pursuits to be explored and developed for their worth and intrinsic value. The chosen people of God, living in the holy land as the rulers and religious establishment, are represented in this elder son. They had become so infatuated with their privileges and wealth that bearing the name of God and holding their sacred office turned into a profitable commodity. They no longer viewed the connections to their people as a responsibility towards their kindred, but only as a duty to preserve their growing enterprises. It's not the same to work for a boss as to partner in business with your father; it's not the same to help an acquaintance as to invest in the growth of your brother. These details in the story speak to us about how easily we can become dispassionate if our approach to community is merely functional and superficial. I am amazed how we sit today in churches and attempt to celebrate the Lord's banquet surrounded by people that we don't personally know, and don't care to be connected with beyond the interest of some useful personal agenda. The journey back home should inspire brothers and sisters to ask about each other's spiritual well-being, as members of one spiritual family. We should be asking people with tenderness, "Where have you been? What have you learned from your challenges? Tell me about your story, who are you now in relation to where you have been? What must be healed from the past, and how can we better understand our relationship to do life together?" Imagine what different conversation could take place if we filtered our emotional dissatisfaction through a personal approach to understanding. If we were in the elder brother's shoes, we would confess, "Father, I don't mean to steal the joy of this moment, because I know how much it should mean to us that my brother has returned safely home. Help me forgive the past and process my resentment towards him, so that I can be a part of this special occasion with you and him, not only in action but in heart."

*3. An exaggerated sense of self-importance.* He is a legend in his own mind. This son is pictured as a very hard-working person who is keeping a record of everything he does. He doesn't work out of love, but out of competition, to compare himself to those he esteems as inferior. "I never broke any of your commandments," he said. He has a list of all his accomplishments. In his mind, he can do no wrong.

It is embarrassing to admit that many believers take all the commandments written in the law and, instead of realizing their shortcomings to reach a place of repentance, choose to attempt in their own strength to live up to the standards of righteousness that only God can confer upon those who seek to partake of His process of sanctification. It is astonishing that we can take spiritual exercises like scriptural readings, regular prayers, continual fasting, and even sacramental consumption, and reduce it all to spiritual medals we proudly display upon our pontifical chest. Everything prescribed in the word is designed to expose our spiritual condition, to basically lead us to a place of acknowledgment of our spiritual depletion so that, in humility, we can experience godly remorse. This is a simple yet very hard lesson to learn, and some people spend an entire lifetime without understanding it. The fact that the elder brother can proudly state, "I never broke any of the commandments," ironically invalidates all his accomplishments in that moment, even if it were true. The father did not need any of the son's obedience in order to celebrate his sonship. If all his work and compliance was only an attempt to earn more favor, he misconstrued the relationship with his father and totally misunderstood the intentions of his heart. If obedience produces arrogance instead of affection, and the application of the rules is used as leverage for demands instead of opportunities to display gratitude, this elder son is more lost than his younger brother, even while he has never left the home. The father would say to the son, "My child, I would rather you receive your brother and rejoice with me than obey all the rules of the house and live with a heart empty of love[69]." The countervision Jesus is presenting to national Israel is revolutionary, because it's basically saying that everything transcribed in the Old Testament was supposed to enlighten the people of God to see themselves as members of a troublesome yet dearly beloved family in covenant. No wonder Paul writes, "Owe nothing to anyone except to love and seek the best for one another; for he who [unselfishly] loves his neighbor has fulfilled the [essence of the] law [relating to one's fellowman]. The commandments, 'You shall not commit adultery, you shall not murder, you shall not steal, you shall not covet,' and any other commandments are summed up in this statement: 'You shall love your neighbor as yourself.' Love does no wrong to a neighbor [it never hurts anyone]. Therefore [unselfish] love is the fulfillment of the Law."

The law is not only about what we have done wrong, but about exposing what we have the potential of doing because of our unregenerate hearts. Imagine if I came up to you and said, "Don't steal my car." Your response would probably be, "Who says I want to steal anything?" You would be offended because of the presupposition that you are capable of such a thing. Well, when God says His don't-do commandments, he is literally saying, this is what I see is in you, and you don't have the ability to recognize or see it in yourself because you are still in denial

---

[69] Galatians 6:2, Matthew 7:12, Galatians 5:14.

about the depth of your fallen nature. Commandments are not about proving to God that we are not what he has stated concerning our own depravity. They are not about God shaming us into condemnation to embarrass us about our filth. They are simply a healing conversation designed to lead us into a true loving relationship, one that is committed to bringing supernatural transformation through repentance until we can learn to love others with the same grace we have enjoyed from His covenant faithfulness.

*4. Apparently, this exemplary son felt a hidden discontent with his status.* "In this house," he insinuated, "I never got a shot at happiness." He was quick to resent the loss of a portion of his inheritance. Even when he already had his fair share divided unto him, still he begrudged the loss of his brother's portion. He had not forgotten the past, and was bitter about what had transpired.

The burden of false spirituality is hidden discontent. True spiritual fulfillment will never be found in religious covetousness. The leaders Jesus was addressing in this parable through the character of the elder son had too much to lose in this world to gain anything of true value in the kingdom of God. I often wonder, if I were a multi-millionaire and gave away all my wealth to those I love, how many of them would get closer to me after I shared everything I had with them? I know most people would like to think that all of them would want to give back to my vision, be more connected, and use all of our collective resources to build one another in love. Yet the truth could be very different. I have seen on many occasions that possessions increase hidden aspirations, and suppressed desires get empowered to come to the surface. The elder brother had a taste of the inheritance, and now all he sees is the equity of his savings and investments. He is living as though His Father is dead, craving more of what he envisions one day will be his. The last thing he wants is for someone else to come into the household to take another slice out of his pie. The Father says to the elder son, everything I have is yours, why is that not enough? I am always with you, and you are always at the house. Why don't you even want to share some of that joy with your brother? When we lose our delight in connectedness, we cease to appreciate our privileges with humble gratitude, and end up in a never-ending quest to appease our dissatisfaction with greediness. The celebration of belonging to a family that shares the joys and struggles of life together was the appeal that Jesus made to his accusers, who could not understand why they needed to share the kingdom with undeserving crowds. My greatest joy as a partaker of the elements of communion is to experience the sincerity of caring for all those who share the meal of the Kingdom with me. In that enjoyment there are no more requests, goals, or aspirations, because in the presence of God I can possess everything I ever wanted or needed. Those outside the true experience of the Lord's table will always crave more of the things that don't satisfy, and they will lust for power, recognition, and self-aggrandizement.

*5. He covered his resentment with false humility, disguising his true feelings with hypocrisy.* He was quick to single out the fattest calf, but camouflaged his desire for it, claiming he would have been satisfied with a little calf.

It is amazing how Jesus illustrated the personal thoughts and inner reasonings of the supposedly well-behaved elder sons of Israel. Notice that the younger son basically declared his father as good as dead by claiming his inheritance and leaving the house with it, yet the elder brother was no different than the prodigal. Though he covered his indifference to his father by claiming that he had worked devoutly for many years to please him, the reality was that for all those years he only thought about building his own empire. We know that the elder brother cared little about the disrespect of the younger brother to the father when asking for the portions of goods that belonged to him, because in principle he did the same thing when begrudging the loss of the inheritance of his brother, even accusing his father of wasteful spending in investing in his own son. In other words, he questioned his father's spending habits, arguing about resources as if they were already his. The scripture says the father divided unto both his substance, yet if according to the older son it was so wrong for the father to give his inheritance to the prodigal, why did the elder kept his portion? This elder son was also living as if his father was dead to him, even though he was pretending to be in good standing with him by living in his house.

The younger son said in his heart, "I have sinned against heaven," and "My father, I am not worthy," yet the elder brother says to his father, "I have served faithfully all my life, I gave myself to this house and never have broken any commandments." There is no pretense with the prodigal; he is what he is, and he acknowledges it, but the elder brother covers his frustration and justifies his attitudes by hiding behind his service. Through this parable, Jesus seemed to be subtly exposing that the supposedly spiritual and mature sons of the house of Israel were not as close to the Father as they presumed to be. They appeared all sanctimonious in front of the masses, but the truth was that their hearts had been corrupted and were far from true intimacy with God. Jesus said that the elder brother accused the prodigal of wasting all his money in prostitution, but if you read the anecdote carefully, there is nothing in the text that insinuates any immoral behavior. Here again, though purely devoted to the confines of the father's house, the elder son's mind has wandered in his imagination into depravity and decadence. He has no evidence that what he accuses his brother of actually occurred. What are we to make of his speculations? Is he being overly critical and judgmental, or is Jesus perhaps telling us how the leaders of his time only looked clean in their outward form, but had completely polluted minds? The elder brother in the parable cannot be honest with himself; he really wanted the fattest calf, the whole communal celebration, and all the attention and affection that was bestowed upon his brother, but instead of recognizing his jealousy, he lied about his envy, claiming he thought it was unfair that he was never given a small party for a group of his friends. I have come to learn that the best way to approach a vision of community around the Lord's table is with an attitude of transparency and honesty, both with ourselves and those who commune with us. There is no place for pretention when the Lord seeks to address the reality of the dysfunctions and pollutions that plague our wounded souls.

6. *He is overly skeptical of experiences he hasn't shared or simply doesn't understand.* In his frustration, he attacks his brother; even his father has exposed his cynicism. He attributes hidden motives and agendas to their actions. The picture of a house full of celebration is foreign to

him. He falsely concludes that if he is not experiencing joy, then the joy of others can't be warranted.

Judgmental attitudes are one of the most divisive and destructive issues that separate believers and churches inside the Body of Christ. If we were at a church service and a person walked to the front of the altar and burned $100,000, what would we say about it? We probably would say, "What a waste, that money could have been given to the poor." There is one person in the scriptures that thought the same as we would; his name was Judas. Judas could not relate to the expression of love, and the value of the things he deemed most important to him caused him to attack those who didn't reflect his values. The elder son in the parable cannot conceive of any justifiable reason for wasting such lavish luxuries on a fleeting moment that will soon be forgotten. Worst of all, he cannot relate to anyone being so exuberant about an occasion that he interprets as regrettable and shameful. There are many expressions of faith that are quite different than ours within the household of God. In Christianity, there are many strange expressions of devotion used in different traditions when celebrating heavenly things. We cannot wrongly conclude that just because we never approach God with a certain style of worship, that particular form of adoration must be invalid. Traveling in time, we would see Jesus being known as a glutton and a friend of sinners, since his banquets were perceived as disorderly and socially unacceptable. People who were not supposed to even be at the table were dining in the wrong seats, and everyone was acting glad about it. Many of the traditions Jews hold in the highest esteem were being overlooked and neglected by Jesus and his followers. The elder son of the Father represents a form of national Israel that was deeply offended in Jesus' day. We should imagine the Lord's banquet today as the glorious festivity that brings reconciliation for prodigals and elders alike, celebrating their covenant status within the household of God. We ought to not waste energy criticizing our unique manifestations of devotion, and instead appreciate our common inheritance as members of the same family of God.

7. *The elder brother is basing his identity on his performance, not on his relationships to his family.* "All these years I have served you," he said in self-righteousness. With no care for belonging to his family name or love for his father and brother, he only sees in terms of personal merits and achievements. He wanted a celebration with his friends, and those he surrounded himself with seemed more important than his own family.

We see in this parable that both sons needed a change of heart and a deeper connection to their father. Jesus' unique storytelling depicts the hidden realm of the human heart, because in His sacramental presence, he desires to confront and transform our internal struggles, conflicts, and traumas. Eating and drinking at the Lord's table is more than a simple ritual or religious exercise; this is where we do our family's business, where we rearrange our mindset and change our disposition towards God and others, because every one of us has a little bit of each of these two brothers inside us. The disciples sat around Jesus' Passover celebration as representatives of a new, redefined Israel, and in those roles, they were confronted with the prospects of internal conflict and betrayal. Jesus then announced the difficult news of His imminent death and departure, and later on, Satan entered the midst at the meal scene to wreak havoc in their small community. This was a very intense and dramatic dinner event in every conceivable way. The remembrance of these scenes could not be any more sobering for those observants that re-enacted them. At the Lord's Supper, the veil has been pulled back, and the parables of Jesus have turned into a living reality in front of our own eyes. The storytelling has materialized into a true personal experience, and now we have to become the living characters in God's dynamic drama. The promise of citizenship, the status of constant immigration, the living in a strange land under a foreign government you can never call your own; that's basically the story of the whole Bible. In the scriptures, this illustration represents our spiritual condition before God.

That is why God sympathizes with all those who seek asylum, long for community, and desire the embrace of a family they can belong to; because the Father Himself has always longed for the completion of

His final habitation, and the spiritual edification of the people who will become His ultimate abode and family for the rest of eternity. What a drama—humanity longing for a place to be made their home, and divinity searching for a people that will become His residency.

## *The Father*

We will fail in our exegesis of this parable if we don't address the character of the Father. A very important aspect of eating at the communion table is enjoying the paternal image of God delighting over us. Imagine a location where love is received in the most pure, genuine way. There you find no worries, anxiety, or even fear—only real peace, fullness of joy, and total trust. In that place, absolute security is the dominant experience, and complete rest is the ultimate state of being. There you encounter strength, sustenance, acceptance, and passion that makes you feel fully alive to yourself and the world around. Where are you? Where is such a place? Heaven? Close, but not exactly. We're talking about Jesus' description of the father's house, Christ's dream home for us, the place where heaven and Earth come together in the revelation of the Father experienced around the Lord's table (John 14:2-3). The father's image is one of being a covering of authority for us. That means that when seated at His fellowship table, we should feel protected and sheltered. That is a powerful thought to explore when we are dining together in the presence of God. The father is standing guard over our festivities, and our access to his love and mercies is uninterrupted. The portrayal Jesus gave of the Father is one of extravagance. In the story, he runs towards the son in an undignified manner. He lavishes the prodigal son with gifts and privileges. The father doesn't even allow the son to finish his prepared speech. This could be a cryptic way for Jesus to report that this dad doesn't need to be convinced to restore His own sons back into covenant status. When we partake of the Lord's Supper, that's the humbling picture Jesus wants us to rehearse in our minds. There is nothing to fear; we are finally back home.

Sacramental communion is learning how to abide in that realm of fellowship and intimacy with God until we can experience for ourselves the words of Jesus when he said: "Father I thank you, because you always hear me."[70]

This sacred communion is available; it's been made ready and fully equipped for your accommodation. The Father has no other expectation than continually waiting and making preparations for your arrival and permanent stay. I think it is time we return back home to where we belong. Let us go back to the place of stability, comfort, and safety. Let us return to our spiritual family, and our spiritual home within the Father's house.

---

[70] John 11:41–42.

# 6

# Celebrating the Lord's Supper

## Models of Performance

During my journey of studying sacramental theology, one of the most interesting endeavors was determining how exactly to apply all the principles and truths I learned. It was curious to me how, after much thought and reflection, I ended up with a model very similar to the one practiced by the different traditional churches. The fact that worship must be done in some sort of ceremonial manner had already been established.[71] Now what kind of ceremonial format should be adopted? Choosing all-encompassing rituals that many believers can identify with is a challenge, and it requires a bit of creativity and sensitivity to address all the needs and limitations of the congregation. Eventually I settled in a three-step ceremony that includes the reading of scriptures and the participation of the congregation in each part of the different rites. I present this model only as an example to inspire, and perhaps stimulate, the imagination of all those who desire to reignite their excitement for the remembrance of Jesus' last supper. Perhaps some will adopt a few principles from this model, while others could implement all of them. The main purpose of this chapter is simply to engage in the practical demonstration of all the concepts we have so far covered in our study. I know for me personally, it was a challenge to channel all that I had discovered into a specific model suitable for services. That

---

[71] Jesus, minister of the bread and wine, demonstrated the power and significance of ceremonial rituals.

is why my aim is to provide what I believe can be some useful tips and tools for others to follow.

There are a few scriptural elements that perhaps should never be replaced when organizing or creating a ceremonial celebration of the Lord's Supper:

1. The examining of oneself.
2. The exercise of remembrance.
3. The blessing of the elements.
4. The reading of sacramental scriptures.
5. The giving of thanks.

The way one communicates these five scriptural elements could vary in form, through different kinds of music, forms of prayer, Bible readings, and even symbolic rites. I chose to combine all these elements in the three-step format that we are about to present in this chapter. Let's come into the part of the service in which we would commemorate the Lord's table, discussing this process from beginning to end.

The first challenge one faces is often the question: who is invited to participate? I personally make the invitation to all those present at the congregation; if they choose to do so, everyone is welcomed. Now, no matter how much we teach, preach, or appeal to have everyone join, there are always a few who decide not to participate. That is why, if necessary, a brief announcement is made before the ceremony to dismiss anyone who doesn't desire to be a part of the celebration. To me, having no participants during the activities seems uncomfortable and awkward, to both the congregation and the people who don't partake of the elements.

## Table with a Veil Covering

The first symbolic picture I incorporated in reenacting the Lord's Supper was a table decorated with Biblical allusions to the different meanings of the ceremony. On the table, we place a crown of thorns, nails, grapes, wheat bread, and incense candles, to mention a few. Then we cover the table with a veil, which we later switch to some curtains to represent the holy place being opened on our behalf to enter into God's presence. Maybe for some this would be a little too much, but I am attempting to engage with a culture that is Biblically illiterate, teaching them to think symbolically by making the scriptural narrative as alive as possible to their hearts. During this first step, the scripture would be read:

> *"Now the Festival of Unleavened Bread arrived, when the Passover lamb is sacrificed. Jesus sent Peter and John ahead and said, 'Go and prepare the Passover meal, so we can eat it together.'"*

> *"Jesus said, 'I have been very eager to eat this Passover meal with you before my suffering begins. For I tell you now that I won't eat this meal again until its meaning is fulfilled in the Kingdom of God.'" (Luke 22:7-8, 15-16 NLT)*

After the reading of these scriptures, I say the words, "Today we prepared the table of the Lord in remembrance of Jesus, and we declared that the fulfillment of this Passover has already been accomplished at the cross. Therefore, we are already eating with Him at His kingdom as we celebrate this table of communion." Sometimes after the reading of these words, I would further elaborate, "As the disciples prepared the table, we are preparing our hearts," or pray something along those lines.

Then the veil would be opened, and different volunteers from the congregation would come up to the table to light the candles and fill a cup of wine, representing the illustration of disciples preparing their hearts as Peter and John prepared the Passover meal. Another very helpful detail is the timing and choosing of music, which complements the actions of opening the veil and preparing the table very well.

## The Breaking of the Bread

In the second step of the ceremony, the scripture would be read: "As they sat down to eat, he took the bread and blessed it. Then he broke it and gave it to them. Suddenly, their eyes were opened, and they recognized him. And at that moment he disappeared!" (Luke 24:30-31 NLT).

After the reading of this passage, I say, "Jesus disappeared because He is already present with us here in the breaking of bread, that your eyes may be opened like the eyes of the disciples so that you can see Jesus revealed in the elements of this table." Then we would pass loaves of bread around, so that the congregation will reenact Jesus' actions in the breaking of the bread. Often, I will give the example first, modeling how to do the blessing and breaking of the bread to everyone, saying different prayers that they can repeat which confer divine meaning on their actions. This second step is also an allusion to the multiplication of the food by the disciples' hands, representing in God's presence that there is more than enough for all to be satisfied with leftovers. Jesus broke the bread and left it at the table as a sign of new creation; in a similar fashion, we encourage the participants to only break it and put it back in the trait, not to consume it. This serves also as an allusion to the sign of the hidden manna in the holy of holies that was left untouched. After the congregants perform this symbolic act, a loaf of bread is handed back to the presiding minister, and placed back at the table to illustrate the sign of God's provision. Our servers are usually instructed before each service to remind those who participate how to break the bread and place it back on the trait. If they are struggling to get people to follow the instructions, we encourage the servers to do the process themselves and assist each person if necessary. This portion of the service, if done right, has the most potential to bless all those involved, because it allows everyone to connect to one another and experience the ceremony in unison.

## The Partaking of the Elements

The last part of the celebration is the reading of the traditional passage of Paul's instructions to the church at Corinth: "For I pass on to you what I received from the Lord himself. On the night when he was betrayed, the Lord Jesus took some bread and gave thanks to God for it. Then he broke it in pieces and said, 'This is my body, which is given for you. Do this in remembrance of me.' In the same way, he took the cup of wine after supper, saying, 'This cup is the new covenant between God and his people—an agreement confirmed with my blood. Do this in remembrance of me as often as you drink it.' For every time you eat this bread and drink this cup, you are announcing the Lord's death until he comes again" (1 Corinthians 11:23-26 NLT).

After reading this passage, I pronounce the words, "Here it is, the blood and the body of the Christ, a perfect offering and eternal sacrifice of worship to the Father on our behalf. Let's worship today with Jesus at His table." Then the elements of bread and wine are distributed among the congregation, and everyone is served. We will usually pray before the consumption of the bread and the wine, and the prayers for each one will vary according to the message that was preached or the specific needs in the congregation that may need addressing. The moment of partaking should be done in silence, pausing for a brief time to allow the reverent occasion to be pondered by everyone present.

## Frequently Asked Questions

One question many inquire about during the celebration of the Lord's Supper is, what exactly is going on when we partake of the elements? Are our actions of eating or drinking purely symbolic, or is there something unique and distinctive taking place that is not applicable to other Christian activities? My personal impression is that there is something exclusive to the rite of communion that is unique to its celebration, and not purely or merely symbolic. The most vivid and clear example is the account of the Corinthians' abuses of the Lord's table. If they conducted the rite incorrectly, and without any proper understanding of its true meaning, one would expect to conclude that their actions would be void of any serious spiritual implications. Yet the opposite is stated by Paul; even while apparently ignorant, their handling of the ritual still carried some significant spiritual weight. Something was manifested in their midst, and they are now accountable for it. The phrase used to describe the mishandling of the rite is unmistakable: "So anyone who eats this bread or drinks this cup of the

Lord unworthily is guilty of sinning against the body and blood of the Lord" (1 Corinthians 11:27 NLT).

The scripture describes our eating and drinking of the kingdom meal as "koinonia" with the blood and the body of Christ. We are not just drinking or eating wine and bread, we are in some sense assimilating the blood and body of the Messiah. Interestingly, the word "koinonia" in the New Testament is used in a very particular manner to describe divine connectivity. With the exception of the times that the word is translated with reference to other occasions, it is indicative of an exchange with the divine nature, with the infusion of God's attributes. Let's see some examples of this word:

- *"God will do this, for he is faithful to do what he says, and he has invited you into partnership with his Son, Jesus Christ our Lord." (1 Corinthians 1:9 NLT)*

The Corinthians, who in this context are described as endowed with every spiritual gift, will be strong and kept blameless because of their (koinonia) partnership. Apparently this "koinonia" partnership is of divine quality, because it is conferring effectual and distinctive grace upon all the congregation.[72]

- *"Be not unequally yoked with unbelievers: for what fellowship have righteousness and iniquity? or what communion hath light with darkness?" (2 Corinthians 6:14 ASV)*

The word translated "communion" is "koinonia"; what transfer or intimate mingling can occur between light and darkness? The answer is none, it is impossible, because their natures are diametrically opposed to one another.[73]

---

[72] 1 John 1:3, another example of Christ's koinonia.
[73] 1 John 1:6, 7. The koinonia disperses darkness with the light, and releases the divine transfer of Christ's propitiation through his blood.

- *"The grace of the Lord Jesus Christ, and the love of God, and the communion of the Holy Spirit, be with you all." (2 Corinthians 13:14 ASV)*

The koinonia with the Holy Spirit is not external, but internal, saturating our innermost being with everything concerning the Godhead. Through the Holy Spirit, we are capable of assimilating spiritually what it means to have an intimate, supernatural relationship with God.[74]

- *"And when they perceived the grace that was given unto me, James and Cephas and John, they who were reputed to be pillars, gave to me and Barnabas the right hands of fellowship, that we should go unto the Gentiles, and they unto the circumcision." (Galatians 2:9 ASV)*

The term "right-hand" is an aphorism for the divine grace imparted for the gifts of consecration and ordination. This was not done as a mere superficial formality, to give away a casual endorsement. This was the spiritual connection and intimate divine impartation that established all the godly elements of the transfer of God's blessings through the Holy Spirit.[75]

Therefore, when the scripture states:

- *"The cup of blessing which we bless, is it not a communion [koinonia] of the blood of Christ? The bread which we break, is it not a communion [koinonia] of the body of Christ?" (1 Corinthians 10:16 ASV)*

---

74 Phillippians 2:1 includes another expression similar to this one.
75 Phillippians 1:5 is another example of the word "koinonia" in this context of spiritual partnership.

This communicates the idea of a substantial, legitimate intermingling of the divine realities of the blood and body of Christ through the actions of eating and drinking. The context of this passage attests to and confirms this fact by later concluding,

- *"And though we are many, we all eat from one loaf of bread, showing that we are one body." (1 Corinthians 10:17 NLT)*

This phrase seems to describe the symbolic illustration of the bread as one solid substance. The allegory reflects on how the natural is transformed into the spiritual. We are many in the natural, yet one in the Spirit; we all partake of the same bread, as if to communicate the idea of being one in the moment of consumption of the bread.

- *"Think about the people of Israel. Weren't they united by eating the sacrifices at the altar?" (1 Corinthians 10:18 NLT)*

Yet again, something was happening spiritually during their connections with the altar. The actions of eating and drinking seem to have real divine ramifications.

- *"I am saying that these sacrifices are offered to demons, not to God. And I don't want you to participate with demons." (1 Corinthians 10:20 NLT)*

The argument in this section is basically opening our minds to the possibility that through the word "koinonia," the apostle is showing us that something divine is being contacted through the elements of communion, in the same category of spiritual realities mentioned throughout the scriptures when the same word "koinonia" is used. These things are the ones already mentioned above, like the gifts of Christ, the internal intimacy with the Holy Spirit, and the supernatural commission enabling us to fulfill God's work.

## *The Idealist vs. The Realist?*

Another question that could appear simple on the surface: "Is it really necessary to celebrate the Lord's Supper? Isn't more important to be the body of Christ than to perform a ritual that many people may not understand anyway?" I have come to learn that there are certain things in life that, even though they could be true in principle, don't really become fully a part of us until we actually express them in practice. Imagine a couple that, even though they are in a relationship together, never really communicate or actually commit their love to each other. Is it enough for them to say, "We know in our hearts that we are together, so there is no need to express it?" I would argue that such a couple has a very limited, undeveloped experience of the full potential and depth of a relationship. When we gather at a certain place and time, doing very particular things with specific people, we experience things together that could never really have become a part of us until we had fully expressed them. It is very interesting to observe how many educated Christians and new converts alike, when confronted with a simple declaration over a piece of bread, are suddenly awakened to realize how things they understood in theory are now seen in a completely different light through practice. When you reverently hold the cup of blessings in your hands, and you sit at the disciples' place in a reenactment of the Lord's Supper, it shakes you to the very core of your being. In the experience of hearing His words, "This is the cup of the new covenant in my blood which is poured out for you," then we literally relive the power of that moment in His very presence. The question then becomes more clear: am I really in the Lord's vision? Are the people around me as meaningful to me as they were to the Lord? There are things God will communicate with His people that perhaps can only be understood in that particular unique and personal experience.

## *Ministering to the Lord at the Table*

We are ministers of the new covenant that administers the bread and wine of the Lord. According to Hebrews 10:5, Jesus' incarnation prepared a way for God to resume and consummate all the old covenant sacrifices into one single offering, which is now commemorated within the ministry and fellowship of His people. The believers that belong to God's family create an atmosphere of connectivity with God, and restore the image of God inside their hearts. In the presence of God, we should be able to express the nature and character of Christ with forgiveness, reconciliation, and restoration. The glory that was only accessible to one man in the Old Testament is now accessible to the corporate man in the New Testament. The responsibilities of the administration of God's house, which were confined to one priestly family, are now distributed among all the household of God, who are made kings and priests in the reign of Christ's kingdom. This new dispensation of grace opens the way for a variety of fresh expressions of faith. The common participation of all believers sharing in the fullness of the Spirit gave opportunities to all Christians to minister unto the Lord as one.

> *"Well, my brothers and sisters, let's summarize. When you meet together, one will sing, another will teach, another will tell some special revelation God has given, one will speak in tongues, and another will interpret what is said. But everything that is done must strengthen all of you." (1 Corinthians 14:26 NLT)*

> *"Don't be drunk with wine, because that will ruin your life. Instead, be filled with the Holy Spirit, singing psalms and hymns and spiritual songs among yourselves, and making music to the Lord in your hearts. And give thanks for everything to God the Father in the name of our Lord Jesus Christ." (Ephesians 5:18-20 NLT)*

> *"Let the message about Christ, in all its richness, fill your lives. Teach and counsel each other with all the wisdom he gives. Sing psalms and hymns and spiritual songs to God with thankful hearts. And whatever you do or say, do it as a representative of the Lord Jesus, giving thanks through him to God the Father." (Colossians 3:16-17 NLT)*

Special attention should be given to the way in which the church was able to keep their unity and Christ-centered vision within this format of free spiritual expression coming from all believers. If psalms are understood as inspired, sacred songs of exaltation, and the book of Psalms contains spontaneous singing that is led by the Spirit, then the important link between these two activities would be the hymns. The hymns, like the psalms, are songs of exaltation that could derive from the scriptures but are not limited to the book of Psalms. They are interpretative songs that merge the two worlds of spontaneous expression, spiritual songs and the Biblical foundation of God's instructive revelation. When the Christian banquet is celebrated with the focus on the exaltation of Christ, and the Eucharist is at the center of this revelation, it makes sense that hymns are sung in the symposium part of the banquet. These singing activities would be useful as instruction on the proper form of worship within the Christian meetings. Notice some of the few hymns recorded in the New Testament, and the way they illuminate our understanding of Christ's vision in the church's participation of Him in the sacramental elements.

*"Without question, this is the great mystery of our faith: Christ was revealed in a human body and vindicated by the Spirit. He was seen by angels and announced to the nations. He was believed in throughout the world and taken to heaven in glory." (1 Timothy 3:16 NLT)*

*"Though he was God, he did not think of equality with God as something to cling to. Instead, he gave up his divine privileges; he took the humble position of a slave and was born as a human being. When he appeared in human form, he humbled himself in obedience to God and died a criminal's death on a cross. Therefore, God elevated him to the place of highest honor and gave him the name above all other names, that at the name of Jesus every knee should bow, in heaven and on earth and under the earth, and every tongue declare that Jesus Christ is Lord, to the glory of God the Father." (Philippians 2:6-11 NLT)*

These songs are theologically and doctrinally rich; they enhance the experience of honoring the exalted Christ as a humble servant, and like the elements themselves on the table, they have come in a simple form that humanity can understand. In the moment of worship, many will be challenged to realize that the ways we underestimate the Lord's body in sacramental and corporal form are the very same ways Jesus' humanity was rejected and overlooked on Earth. While enthralling songs have been sung to the triumph of the cross and the victory through the blood, believers are encouraged not to undervalue the Lord's Supper as the source of true nourishment for their souls. They are admonished to not make the same mistakes the world made by ignoring the propitiation and reconciliation offered through Jesus' sacrificial death. This salvation is not obvious to the senses; in many ways, it is anathema to our fallen nature. The blood and body must be discerned by the hymn, which brings revelation to the true message of the gospel. How are we singing to the Lord today? Do we honor songs that are sacramental in nature, like the ones celebrated in the early hymns of the Church?

> *"The message of the cross is foolish to those who are headed for destruction! But we who are being saved know it is the very power of God." (1 Corinthians 1:18 NLT)*

> *"So when we preach that Christ was crucified, the Jews are offended and the Gentiles say it's all nonsense. But to those called by God to salvation, both Jews and Gentiles, Christ is the power of God and the wisdom of God." (1 Corinthians 1:23-24 NLT)*

## The Ethics of Heaven

Could it be that one of the reasons the Lord instituted the breaking of the bread and the giving of thanks in the cup of the new covenant is to teach us how to behave according to the protocols and ordinances of heaven on Earth? Maybe some of these rules and commandments are not simply to create alignment or obedience to the dictates of authority, but instead to awaken our spiritual senses to the realities that cannot be enjoyed unless our hearts are perceptive to corporal dynamics. There is one unavoidable message in communion that cannot be mistaken, and that is congregational worship. Our collective time of unity and togetherness, shared in the presence of God, creates a unique opportunity to exercise faith for the vision of becoming one body. We come to the presence of God to celebrate the very specific visitation, treatment, and involvement of God in our communal life. Let's carefully examine how the sacramental liturgy opens our hearts to discern the spiritual order of community in a way that is impossible in any other context. Here, we will see some church fathers describing the experience of each congregation as the incarnation of the extension of Christ and the apostles in our relationships on Earth. These quotes show us that *saying we want the leading of the Holy Spirit without any association with human leadership is like saying we want the covering of God the Father without following the example of obedience of His Son.* The sacraments regulate our attitudes in a posture of submission.

> *"I exhort you to study to do all things with divine harmony. The bishop presides in the place of God, and the presbyters in the place of the assembly of the apostles." (Ignatius)*

> *"According to my opinion the grades here in the church are imitations of the angelic glory and of that arrangement which awaits those who follow in the footsteps of the apostles." (Clement of Alexandria)*

> *"Be subject to the presbyters and deacons as unto God and Christ." (Polycarp)*

Here we see how eating and drinking in the meal of the Kingdom educates our senses to better handle the conventions and ethics of heavenly realities. It is a way of protecting us from disconnecting the correct disposition of our hearts from the activities and exercises we display as our spiritual responsibilities. No one will serve at a banquet with the vestments of a trash collector, or invite your former lovers to dinner with your fiancé to celebrate your engagement. These things sound so counterintuitive, yet for God's banquet we sometimes leave all common sense behind. I was at a Christian theme park one day, participating at a play of the last supper of Jesus. In this particular presentation, we as the audience would share in the dramatization of the performance by taking of the communion, along with the actors playing the disciples. The room was closed, the lights were turned off and we were instructed to close our eyes. Suddenly, when we were told to open our eyes, Jesus appeared standing in the midst of the table, looking straight at us. This particular actor portraying Jesus was really going out of his way to try to convey that we were, at that moment, dining with the Lord. Let me tell you something: I think that whole experience, hearing the words of Jesus spoken over us as if it was the Lord Himself, is probably the most accurate portrayal of the true communion service God desires for our lives. I left that presentation with a deep sense of awe and appreciation for the power of the Lord's Supper. I think that is exactly what our communion experience should be: a complete dramatization of the last moments of the Lord on Earth, until Jesus Himself becomes real to us at His table. The reverential treatment and solemn approach to the splendor of God is communicated to us by our response to the Eucharist. That is why we should respect its power and uphold its protocols in honor.

# 7

# Melchizedek's Blessing

There is a very powerful story in the Old Testament that cannot go overlooked when discussing the Lord's Supper. We are referring to the encounter of Abram with the figure called Melchizedek. A lot has been said about the different possibilities of who he might have been, and our objective in this book will be to focus not primarily on his identity, but instead on what he represents in the discussions regarding the meal of the Kingdom[76]. The life of the patriarch Abram was changed forever after his encounter with this priestly figure. Before their meeting, there is no record of Abram offering sacrifices, or calling on God in covenant fashion. Yet after the blessing of Melchizedek, a new world of intimacy with God was opened to him. He began having supernatural encounters, his name was changed to Abraham, and

---

[76] The problem with the identification of Melchizedek is mainly centered around a few verses in Hebrews:

> *"There is no record of his father or mother or any of his ancestors—no beginning or end to his life. He remains a priest forever, resembling the Son of God.*
>
> *The priests who collect tithes are men who die, so Melchizedek is greater than they are, because we are told that he lives on." (Hebrews 7:3, 8 NLT)*
>
> *"Jesus became a priest, not by meeting the physical requirement of belonging to the tribe of Levi, but by the power of a life that cannot be destroyed. And the psalmist pointed this out when he prophesied, "You are a priest forever in the order of Melchizedek."" (Hebrews 7:16-17 NLT)*

*(Continued)*

he offered sacrifices to God in a new, priestly manner. The mantle of priesthood had been imparted to the patriarch Abram after the king of righteousness gave him his special blessing. The book of Psalms seems to pick up this motif—the priestly blessing of the king of Salem—when it states that the Messiah will have an eternal priesthood according to the order of Melchizedek. This passage in the book of Psalms contains the Old Testament scripture which is quoted most often throughout the New Testament.

> *"The Lord said to my Lord, 'Sit in the place of honor at my right hand until I humble your enemies, making them a footstool under your feet.'" (Psalms 110:1 NLT)*

We therefore know this Melchizedek text is of enormous importance for the early development of the theology of the first Christian church. What is so significant about it? The book of Hebrews seems to shed some light on the manner.

---

[76] *(Continued)* Are these descriptions playful exegesis of the allegorical interpretations of the Genesis 14 and Psalms 110 accounts? Or are these actual beliefs of the author of Hebrews about the nature and identity of this character? The ambiguity of these verses has left the door open for many fanciful interpretations. Many conclude that the safest way to look at these verses is to say that the author of Hebrews is saying that since Genesis don't have a record of lineage for Melchizedek, that means there are priesthoods that don't require such credentials for authenticity. They are directly from God; therefore they don't expire, but remain forever. In this sense, they are resemblances of the Son of God in the old covenant (Hebrews 5:4-6). That is a perfectly sensible way to look at these texts, yet still for many the flexibility of the wording in Hebrews leaves space for curiosity and speculation.

Some say Melchizedek was Christ Himself, while others believe him to be the Holy Spirit manifested in human form in the Old Testament. There are still others who claim Melchizedek was like Adam, a man created separate from the original human race who never partook of the fall. The number of theories such as these are endless, all because of the difficulties of reconciling Hebrews' account of Melchizedek being a man with his description of bearing eternal resemblance to the Son of God.

*"There is no record of his father or mother or any of his ances-
tors—no beginning or end to his life. He remains a priest forever,
resembling the Son of God." (Hebrews 7:3 NLT)*

Two things are mentioned in this text that highlight the importance
of Melchizedek's blessing. Number one: this priesthood resembles
Christ. Number two: this type of ministry is concerned with eternal
matters. Somehow, before there was the cross, a temple, a Levitical
system, or any ordinances of the Mosaic law, there was already the
bread and wine of the Kingdom of God on Earth. How can this be?
If we look at the book of Genesis as a narrative of origins, we will
discover that everything that God was going to unfold through the
progressive revelation of the scriptures was already prophesied from
the beginning in typological form. In other words, the names, places,
events, and characters in the Genesis account contain secret codes that,
when unpacked, will uncover the hidden truths and mysteries of the
kingdom of God.

*"Only I can tell you the future before it even happens. Everything
I plan will come to pass, for I do whatever I wish." (Isaiah
46:10 NLT)*

With this principle in mind, let's look carefully at the bread and
wine inside the Genesis account of Melchizedek's priesthood.

*"After Abram returned from his victory over Kedorlaomer and all
his allies, the king of Sodom went out to meet him in the valley of
Shaveh (that is, the King's Valley). And Melchizedek, the king of
Salem and a priest of God Most High, brought Abram some bread
and wine. Melchizedek blessed Abram with this blessing: 'Blessed
be Abram by God Most High, Creator of heaven and earth. And
blessed be God Most High, who has defeated your enemies for you.'
Then Abram gave Melchizedek a tenth of all the goods he had
recovered." (Genesis 14:17-20)*

If God truly foretells the end from the beginning, then this story is addressing more than what might be initially clear. This is a prophetic picture, illustrating the end-time gathering of the nations (valley of the kings). We see here the blessing of the one whose seed will reclaim the disinherited nations (Abram). Remember, the nations were delegated under the administration of lesser divine beings back in Genesis 11, and now we see the presence of God circulating around a man who will be known as the father of those apostate kingdoms. We also glimpse a foreshadowing of the ultimate spiritual battle between light and darkness. It seems that Abram's rescue mission of his nephew Lot became an apocalyptic event, which shifted or agitated principalities and powers, and provoked the universal priesthood of Melchizedek to come onto the scene. How does God intervene to seal the victory and bless Abram eternally? The bread and wine of the kingdom.

Let's then break this code down. Here we have the king of righteousness (Melchizedek), ruler over the domain of peace (Salem), blessing the exalted father (Abram) and symbolically reenacting the ritual that conceals the spiritual truth of the repossessing of the Earth back to God (bread and wine). The blessing Abram is receiving is not limited to a tribal deity. This mysterious blessing pertains to the new creation in God's future, where there will be no ethnic or gender distinctions, for God will be forever in all. This vision Abram is about to engage goes beyond his own time, and it explains why Hebrews says that Abraham was looking for a city whose maker and builder is God. He was living in tents as a stranger and a foreigner on the Earth, searching for a city with eternal foundations. Somehow, according to Hebrews, Abraham even believed that God could raise his son Isaac from the dead. Even when Isaac was about to be consumed and burned up in sacrifice, he believed God could bring him back. Jesus himself said Abraham saw my day and he rejoiced[77]. Where did Abraham get so much inside knowledge about

---

[77] John 8:56.

God's eternal Kingdom? It all started with Melchizedek's blessing. The grace that is upon Melchizedek is to be the mediator of El Elyon, the God Most High or the Most High God. This name is a technical term used to describe the covenant relationship between God and His divine council. In fact, this specific name is not only mentioned for the first time in this passage, it is also repeated on four different occasions within the span of these few verses. What is this name, El Elyon, trying to convey in these important scriptures? If we accept the premise that Melchizedek is the mediator (priest) of El Elyon (the lord of the council), this king is certifying that Abram has the authority to operate beyond the spiritual boundaries of his day. The king of righteousness, or the king of right standing, is aligning Abram to the covenant faithfulness of the Most High. Therefore, the bread and wine serve here as an illustration that there is no time in eternal matters. Just as Jesus can proclaim the body as broken even though he had not gone to the cross yet, and pronounce the blood as shed while it is still in His veins, we can have Koinonia with an event that took place in the past and unite it to the reality of the cross, as if it were still accessible in the present. We see Melchizedek and Abram partaking of the Lamb of God, which was slain from before the foundations of the world. Notice an important feature often overlooked in this particular story. The king of righteousness is standing in the place of the Most High, the possessor or redeemer of heaven and Earth, to bless Abram.

This expression is effectively saying to Abram, "The creator and rightful owner of all things is purchasing back the Earth and the heavens to reconcile all things to His original design." Melchizedek is saying to Abram, you are empowered, protected, and endowed with miraculous grace, because I stand in the place of the Lord of the council to confirm that you are participating in God's redemptive program of new creation. The king of Salem (peace, well-being) is saying to the future father of kings and many nations, "Here is the evidence of this covenant mediation between the Most High and you. I am bringing the bread and wine, the food of the world to come."

Furthermore, in scripture we see that priests not only stand in the place of God for men, they also stand in the place of men for God[78]. Therefore, in this priestly transaction Melchizedek says a blessing for God in Abram's stead: "Blessed be God Most High who defeated your enemies for you." In this moment Abram unites himself with this king of righteousness in his covenant mediation. That is why he gave up the ambition for power, the honor of men, the reputation of the world, and all the systems of control of his day to embrace the Melchizedek

---

[78] There are a few things that seem to be consistent in the scriptures with regards to Melchizedek. Apparently, as far as we can tell, he was always described or presumed to be a man. That is the only way he could stand as a mediator for human beings (Hebrews 5:1). There seems to be no hint, particularly in the Old Testament, about him being a divine being. Other than his name, which some believe to be actually a title, very little could be taken to speculate he is not from Earth. We know also that Salem was an actual location within the Canaanite region, which many believe to be the origin of ancient Jerusalem. Perhaps the only way to bring Melchizedek close to a divine status is to speculate that while he was a man that was the king of earthly Salem, he also was spiritually the honorary priest of the heavenly Jerusalem. The other thing that seems to be secure within the Biblical narrative is Melchizedek's name as a description of a particular person. Whether interpreted as a title or his actual name, he is always identified and distinguished as a specific individual. In other words, he is never implied to be anybody else other than himself. The only thing that one seems to have available to try to work out any specifics about his identity as a human being is his actual role as a priest and his personal name as a title. There is not much room to work his identity with that little information; nevertheless, the author of Hebrews found plenty to say about Melchizedek with arguments from silence.

order of worship[79]. Instead of taking the spoils of war for himself, he returned all possessions to their original owners and gave a tenth of all the spoils to this king of Salem. In this simple insight, we can glimpse how the true eternal covenant is always mediated by the Christlike priesthood that is administering the sacramental bread and wine of the Kingdom.

The king-priest model seemed to be presented in Melchizedek as the ideal and most superior form of spiritual order. The reason for this preeminence could be derived from the fact that this dual function was always God's original design, from the creation of Adam to the coming of the Son of God. In the New Testament, we are called to be like Jesus, kings and priests according to the order of Melchizedek. That means we should all be ministers of the bread and wine of the Kingdom of God. I see in the blessing of Abram a discipleship in Kingly priesthood, resuming the liturgical process that worshipers must learn in their administration of the presence of God. In other words, the bread and wine are in a sense the embodiment and consummation of the entirety of the future Levitical priesthood. We see the guilt and sin offering typified in Genesis 15:9 by illustrating all the species of

---

[79] Something peculiar about the name "Melchizedek" is that "Zedek," which is translated "righteousness," was also known in ancient times as a recognized deity in the Canaanite region. If Melchizedek is not just a proper name of a person, but also a title attributed to this priest of the most high God, that means that potentially the name of the deity Zedek was encrypted in the title of the king of Salem as a record or trophy of the victory of YHWH as the supreme God in the city of Salem. Since the name "Melchizedek" is viewed theologically in scripture in a positive light, that means Zedek was somehow historically absorbed into YHWH as part of one of His divine attributes describing His nature. The righteousness of God is a prominent feature of God's divine action in the scriptures. This would not be strange, for it was common practice that when a region was converted into the worship of YHWH as their true God, then the names of the foreign deities were incorporated into the worship of YHWH as descriptive attributes of His divine nature. For example, Zedek would cease to be recognized as a god that is to be worshiped, and instead become the zedek of YHWH, or the righteousness of the true most high God (El Elyon). In other words, since YHWH was now recognized as the most High God (El Elyon), all other inferior beings are reduced to mere descriptions of his attributes.

animals that are supposed to be offered in the tabernacle of Moses. In that divine encounter, God Himself in a theophany appears walking amongst the blood of the divided animals. The fire for sacrifices is in His hand, and the smoking furnace where worship will be executed is carried by no other than Himself. It is the Lord alone who will fulfill the divine protocol of worship. He will deal with all the sin and restore the complete consequences of the fall by His own covenant merits, which will be displayed in the incarnation of the eternal Son of God.

> *"That is why, when Christ came into the world, he said to God, 'You did not want animal sacrifices or sin offerings. But you have given me a body to offer. You were not pleased with burnt offerings or other offerings for sin. Then I said, 'Look, I have come to do your will, O God— as is written about me in the Scriptures.' First, Christ said, 'You did not want animal sacrifices or sin offerings or burnt offerings or other offerings for sin, nor were you pleased with them' (though they are required by the law of Moses). Then he said, 'Look, I have come to do your will.' He cancels the first covenant in order to put the second into effect. For God's will was for us to be made holy by the sacrifice of the body of Jesus Christ, once for all time." (Hebrews 10:5-10 NLT)*

The true mediation and ultimate redemption that will repossess the heavens and the earth back to God was executed in the body of Jesus, the Messiah. That is what Abram symbolically witnessed in the fiery torch and smoking oven. The Father and the Son entered into a covenant agreement to bless Abram and his descendants, both in the natural and spiritual seed. This revelation went back to the original meal offering shared with Melchizedek with more clarity and focus. The bread and wine unite us to the remission of all sins, and connect us to the future restitution of all things that were fallen in creation. We can see how in Melchizedek's blessing, not only the meal offering, allows the fulfillment of the guilt and sin offering; furthermore, God Himself comes to have fellowship with Abraham in Genesis 18:6-8, typifying the peace offering. Perhaps one of the most revolutionary ideas ever conceived by human beings is illustrated in this event. The God of the scriptures is embodied, enjoys fellowship, and even eats. Food is seen as something sacred, profoundly spiritual, and reverent in the Bible, so much so that the God of creation partakes of it. Dining with God is becoming one with Him, entering into an intimate covenant relationship. Abraham learned a lot from the partnership of the priestly bread and wine of Melchizedek. He grasped the important concept that one of the most essential parts of having divine communion with God is adequately hosting His presence. The sharing of a meal ultimately seals all transactions in the eyes of this covenant God. So what does Abraham do when visited by the manifestation of YHWH Himself? He presents the willing, free gift of the peace offerings of friendship. Interesting that God calls Abraham His friend in several parts of the scriptures.

> *"But as for you, Israel my servant, Jacob my chosen one, descended from Abraham my friend..."* (Isaiah 41:8 NLT)

> *"O our God, did you not drive out those who lived in this land when your people Israel arrived? And did you not give this land forever to the descendants of your friend Abraham?"* (2 Chronicles 20:7 NLT)

> *"And so it happened just as the Scriptures say: 'Abraham believed God, and God counted him as righteous because of his faith.' He was even called the friend of God."* (James 2:23 NLT)

All five types of offerings that were instructed to be observed in the tabernacle of Moses are illustrated throughout Abram's life. After the peace offering of Genesis 18, it culminates with the burnt offering of Isaac in Genesis 22:2. My main purpose in this section is simply to reflect on how God's dealing with Abraham is a direct result of Melchizedek's blessing, communicated through the sacramental picture of the bread and wine. I believe what was conveyed in Genesis 14:17 was more than complimentary refreshments. The entire passage encodes secrets that confirmed that something divine was being established. Once Abraham received these blessings, a series of supernatural events began to unfold in his life. These divine encounters shed light on the mystery of the meal of which he partook with the King of righteousness. The Melchizedek blessing is the priestly and kingly dominion of the Lord of the council, giving us the kingdom meal that repossessed the heavens and the Earth back to God. The fruit of this blessing is nothing less than the revelation of God Himself, in all His glory, through the elements of the bread and wine. The Melchizedek priesthood is the order in which Jesus operates. That is why the eternal Son of God came to give us His body and blood in the new covenant. In other words, the Lord has delegated to us his kingly priesthood, which releases His complete divine nature. Let us meditate on this profound truth and press deeper into the glory of the meal of the Kingdom of God.

## Relating to the Triune God in Communion

There is a powerful mystery in the liturgical format of standing as Christ in the administration of His body to His church. Dramatizing the complete revelation of divinity, which was illustrated in the sacrifice of the cross, is transformative for the one officiating the rite of communion. When we stand as Christ, presenting the experience of Jesus' body in a sacramental manner, we mystically engage with the assimilation of the relationship inside the fullness of God. We serve at the table in the same manner that Jesus did as he was illustrating the Father to his disciples. We perform as actors the self-emptying of Jesus at the table, and prophecy through the ritual the filling of all things through His Spirit. It seems as though one of the main ways God invites us to His unity in diversity is not necessarily by systematizing the language of persons into a Trinitarian formula, but by immersing us in the experience of interrelation inside the Godhead through expression and emulation. This is very similar to the account of Abraham we examined previously in Chapter One, when God invited the patriarch to step into His shoes in the act of giving up his son. In ritual, we act in Christ's stead, standing as the Son of God in relation to the Father and the Spirit, enjoying the privileged vantage point that reveals the salvific action of God towards us. By allowing us to express love inside the divine nature, God helps us partake of the essence of the true eternal communion that always existed inside Him. In other words, the triune God Himself is in a sense mediated by sacramental theology. We handle the sacred when we administer the infinite koinonia of the blood and body of Christ.

In doing so, we are managing the transcendent transaction of covenant mediation between the Father and the Son in the power of the Spirit celebrated in the Eucharist. We serve the cup the Father gave to the Son, which will give Him both suffering and glory. We become broken with the Son of God as part of His body in the breaking of bread, remembering his sacrifice for the sake of others, laying our lives down like the Son also gave His life for us. We are releasing and enjoying the purest expression of the Spirit when we partake of the fullness of God in the consumption of the elements. Have you ever wondered what Jesus experienced when He broke the bread? From God's angle, we can imagine that He saw redemptive history, creation, and incarnation displaying covenant faithfulness. He saw the Father giving all in His eternal Word that was made flesh. He beheld the Spirit absorbing full humanity in the flesh of the Son of God. He witnessed the offering of love to the Father from the Spirit, in the unity of many sons coming into glory through the Lamb of God. When we step into Jesus' role at the table, we not only see these dynamics intellectually, we spiritually experience their complexity in worship and practice. Let's see how some of these multifaceted dimensions of communion empower us to enlarge our intimacy with God in the celebration of the Eucharist.

## We Preside Over the Congregation of the Household of God

### Knowing the Father in Relation to the Son

#### Incarnation of the Word in Hearts

God has made His official endowment and empowerment vulnerable to the operation of human and divine agency in partnership through priesthood. The leader of a congregation, the head of a family, or the one officiating the sacraments in communion is representing Christ as the Lord represented and revealed the Father. In scripture, there seems to be a spiritual intertwining between believers and their leadership. The way Paul portrays his associations with the members of the body of Christ describes a deep bond of love and commitment that recalls the language used by the Lord Himself while doing His ministry on Earth[80]. As part of our kingly priesthood, we ought to somehow feel one another in communion, and also experience each other in the presence of God[81]. Notice how the apostle Paul describes his unity with those under his care, attributing their growth and development to their spiritual connection with his unique relationship with God.

> *"Oh, my dear children! I feel as if I'm going through labor pains for you again, and they will continue until Christ is fully developed in your lives." (Galatians 4:19 NLT)*

This verse could illuminate the way in which we are united in the presence of God to truly know the Father in relation to the Son—when we beget the word into humanity and plant the incorruptible seed of God's nature into people's hearts, birthing the maturity and development of the Sons of God. Standing in the place of Christ over His body will introduce the concepts of proper spiritual parenting and the perfecting of sonship within our church context. Let us observe some texts throughout church history that reflect on this phenomenon of interdependence within the Church of Jesus Christ.

> *"Wherever the bishop appears, let the congregation be there also. Just as wherever Jesus Christ is there is the Catholic Church." (Ignatius)*

---

[80] Galatians 6:17, Colossians 1:24, 2 Corinthians 1:3-7, 2 Corinthians 4:10-12, 15, Philippians 2:17.

[81] 1 Corinthians 12:26-27, Romans 12:5, 1 Corinthians 12:12.

*"However, the church does not depart from Christ. And the church consists of those who are people united to the priest. Therefore, you should know that the bishop is in the church and the church is in the bishop. If anyone is not with the bishop, he is not with the church..." (Cyprian)*

*"When then you cast yourself at the brethren's knees, you are handling Christ. You are entertaining Christ. In like manner, when they share tears over you, it is Christ who suffers, Christ who begs the Father for mercy." (Tertullian)*

# We Submit Along with the Son, Giving Ourselves Over to the Father in Sacrifice

## Knowing the Son in Relation to the Father

### Submissive and Passionate Worship

We know the Son in relation to the Father when we, like sons, submit to His will, adopting the eternal humility of the Son of God desiring to bring glory to His name. Perfect worship is knowing the depth of passion of the Son for His Father. When we lift the cup of salvation and break the bread of redemption, we are with Jesus, giving our Father glory. Jesus' main aim on Earth was to exalt and honor his Father in everything he said and did. The bread and wine that represents the incarnated blood and body of Jesus speak to us about how God in the flesh has reconciled all things unto Himself. There is nothing in creation that has not been already resolved through the death and resurrection of the Messiah[82]. Complete surrender and submission to God is one of the main demands of the cross. In our spiritual devotion, we are joining with the exalted Lord, who has executed complete restitution in His loving offering of surrender to the Father's will. We recite Jesus' words as our own and meditate on what Jesus lived by reliving His

---

[82] John 3:14, John 12:32.

commitment to us, allowing the Holy Spirit to align our sentiments in synergy with the heart of the Son for the Father.

> *"And because we are his children, God has sent the Spirit of his Son into our hearts, prompting us to call out, 'Abba, Father.'"*
> *(Galatians 4:6 NLT)*

# We Reveal Christ as We Present Him Through the Elements

## Knowing the Spirit in Relation to the Son

### Revelatory Manifestations

As we seek to reveal Christ through the elements, we exercise faith in the activity of the Holy Spirit in the lives of believers. We trust that the Spirit of the living God will open our hearts and minds, to make the partaking of the table a living witness of the truth of the gospel, so everyone can see the glory of God in the face of Jesus Christ. In doing so, we know the Spirit in relation to the Son, when we see the exaltation of the Messiah in the hearts of the believers. All that the Spirit does is reveal more of Jesus! We understand the dynamic interaction of the Spirit with the Son in the distribution of the gifts of the Spirit, and the operations of the different ministries inside the church. All that these gifts and ministries do is express more of the Son of God. Words of knowledge, words of wisdom, and discernment of spirits are synonymous with thinking with the supernatural mind of Jesus. The gifts of faith, healing, and miracles are the empowerment of the Holy Spirit, so we can walk on Earth with the same grace that Jesus displayed in His earthly ministry. The gifts of tongues, interpretations, and prophecy allow us to express the voice of God on Earth in Christ's stead[83]. *Often, God is not as concerned with us hearing revelations as He is interested in us allowing His voice to find expression through our lives.* Jesus is our evangelist, apostle, prophet, teacher, and shepherd, imparted to our faith as we partake of his divine nature in the Eucharist.[84]

---

[83] 2 Corinthians 2:17, 2 Corinthians 4:2, 2 Corinthians 12:19.
[84] 1 Corinthians 12:4-11.

## The Glory of Unity in Diversity Is Celebrated as We All Become One in the Spirit

### Knowing the Spirit in Relation to the Father

#### Offering of Unity in Love

The Spirit unites because He is the unifier who teaches us about harmony.[85] The Spirit sets our example of oneness in how the Father is in the Son and the Son is in the Father[86]. We know the Spirit in relation to the Father when we seek the love of God in our hearts, to bring us to the bond of unity, fellowship, and community[87]. The Spirit eternally unites the Father and the Son, and that union is absorbed and emulated by believers when the Spirit unites us in grace and love. The Spirit knows that the heart of the Father is the unity of His family, so He longs to saturate our souls with the reality of His eternal love[88]. The partaking of the elements has a very powerful focus: bringing all things together in reconciliation and forgiveness. As the Holy Spirit was sent from heaven as the parakletos, we allow Him to express this sentiment and plead for restoration when we voice His concerns for the unity of His body. The sacraments unite the people to God and release all burdens of spiritual debt in unforgiveness.

> *"And all of this is a gift from God, who brought us back to himself through Christ. And God has given us this task of reconciling people to him. For God was in Christ, reconciling the world to himself, no longer counting people's sins against them. And he gave us this wonderful message of reconciliation. So we are Christ's ambassadors; God is making his appeal through us. We speak for Christ when we plead, 'Come back to God!' For God made Christ, who never sinned, to be the offering for our sin, so that*

---

[85] John 16:13.
[86] John 14:10-11, John 14:16, 20.
[87] Ephesians 4:2-4.
[88] Romans 5:5.

*we could be made right with God through Christ." (2 Corinthians 5:18-21 NLT)*

## The Priestly Re-Enactment of the Eternal Covenant

### Knowing the Father in Relation to the Spirit

#### Mediating Atmospheres of Glory

We know the Father in relation to the Spirit when we consecrate our lives, seeking purity and holiness to be presented as a bride to the Son of God. Priesthood upholds the language of covenant, which lays out the stipulations for a relationship. There is a beautiful picture from scripture of the whole of creation entering into marriage with the creator, and mankind standing as the officiating priests that mediate this covenant transaction. The creator Himself modeled priesthood to Adam by joining man and woman into the institution of marriage, showing man how to speak order out of chaos and fashion beauty from emptiness. Adam now is exhorted to imitate God by multiplying His image, protecting the garden, and summoning the praises of creation back to God in priestly worship. In the New Testament, the Father desires a glorious church to be presented to His Son, so He sends the Spirit to prepare us for the coming of the bridegroom. We must be as that covering Father, who releases the Spirit to create the atmosphere of intimacy and communicates the prophetic love letters to prepare the environment for true worship. The language of priesthood is understood in the context of the tabernacle of worship, in which the mediators administer different atmospheres of glory. Everything we do in the power of the Holy Spirit is to supervise the administration of sacred things, like prayer and scripture reading. What is the correct attitude that believers should reflect in the presence of God? What kind of response does God require from us as partakers of the divine nature when His glory is extended towards us with blessings? We as priestly fathers work alongside the Spirit to release the different dimensions of spiritual connectivity, ensuring proper alignment to the different manifestations of God. We say the correct words for people that they cannot say for themselves. We stand as the people, embracing their needs, pain, and difficulties, absorbing them as our own to feel and release their breakthrough in the presence of God. We convey and express adequately what they cannot properly explain in their own language, and the Holy Spirit transfers our effective intercession into their hearts. The Lord's table is the perfect opportunity to explore and uphold these dynamics. We all sense, behold, and express the intention of the Spirit together to enjoy more of His fullness.

> *"For the Lord is the Spirit, and wherever the Spirit of the Lord is, there is freedom. So all of us who have had that veil removed can see and reflect the glory of the Lord. And the Lord—who is the Spirit—makes us more and more like him as we are changed into his glorious image." (2 Corinthians 3:17-18 NLT)*

## We Remember the Human Pain of the Son of God

### Knowing the Son in Relation to the Spirit

**Intercession and Brokenness**

We know the Son in relation to the Spirit when we partake of the mantle of intercession that the Son communicates to the Holy Spirit. Part of the reason why the Word became flesh was to relate the humanity of the eternal son of God to each one of us in a deeper, more intimate way. The humanity of Jesus feels each one of us in all of our distress, trauma, and struggles. God knows it is easier to open up to someone who understands you and feels what you are currently living because they have been in your place. In communion, we not only stand in the place of God to imitate Him, we also reflect on how God stands in our place, taking upon Himself all the burdens of humanity. That is why we open up to Him in such a special way in the partaking of the bread. In the heavenly places, Jesus is taking all of our tears and psychological dysfunctions and transforming them into altars of revelation through His intercession.

> *"Who then will condemn us? No one—for Christ Jesus died for us and was raised to life for us, and he is sitting in the place of honor at God's right hand, pleading for us." (Romans 8:34 NLT)*

The Holy Spirit inside us receives the intercession of Jesus and makes it our own. That is why we become more human in communion than any other religious exercise. At the table of Jesus, we are opening up to our true selves by knowing the intimate understanding God has of us through the sufferings of His Son.

> *"And the Holy Spirit helps us in our weakness. For example, we don't know what God wants us to pray for. But the Holy Spirit prays for us with groanings that cannot be expressed in words. And the Father who knows all hearts knows what the Spirit is saying, for the Spirit pleads for us believers in harmony with God's own will." (Romans 8:26-27 NLT)*

The groaning that cannot be uttered is the human conversation of the Son imparted to the Spirit in an expression of eternal love towards the Father. *In the presence of God, the heart must be broken before the mind can be informed, because divine thoughts are perfected through the inspirational pain of inarticulate groaning.* The time of remembrance of Jesus' sacrifice should be a moment of great spiritual intercession. Not only looking back at the cross for the reenactment of its power, but looking presently to the exalted Christ, who still pleads our case before the Father.

## Concluding Thoughts

We have seen in this section how the administration of the bread and wine presents a unique opportunity to reflect on and experience the different operations of the triune God as they are unfolded as one within the divine nature. The depth of meaning in the ceremony of the partaking of the elements illuminates a world of communion inside God, where all of God can be clearly distinguished in the profound mystery of his divine essence. If one only sees the Lord's Supper as a ritual, the perspective of union with God will not be fully communicated. On the other hand, if we accept the activity of communion as an invitation to stand as God to release YHWH to others, our hearts begin to grasp what it means to know the Father, Son, and Spirit not only in relation to each other, but in expression through us all for each one of us.

# 8

# The Invitation to the Table

## *Sons and Daughters of the Bread and Wine*

The meaning of the Melchizedek priesthood can be understood by the effects it had in the life of Abraham, the recipient of his blessing. The book of Psalms appears to be looking back at the transformation in the life of the patriarch, and concludes that same type of empowerment is the one that will be manifested again on Earth through the life of the Messiah. He will be a King Priest that will transfer his mantle of spiritual covering upon His people.[89] The eternal heavenly priesthood of the Messiah will rise like in Abraham, the fatherhood of nations.[90] The manifestation of the supernatural kingdom of God means the future anointed king of Israel will have the power to reign in the midst of His Enemies.[91] We, being the people of the Messiah, can expect to have that same grace that was upon Abraham by receiving the Melchizedek priesthood that is upon Christ. Every time we administer the bread and wine of the kingdom, we should recall the supernatural encounters of the father of faith, expecting to partake of the same divine visitations. Our identity is transformed into a spiritual covering for others, regardless of their background or nationality. We should trust our commissioning to rule in the midst of the enemies

---

[89] Psalms 110:3.
[90] Psalms 110:6. The meaning and role of Abraham is to bring the model of the fatherhood of God to earth.
[91] Psalms 110:1-2.

of God, and that means experiencing the eternal kingdom while the evil spiritual forces of this world are still trying to delay and oppose the purposes of God. As we saw in the previous chapter, our symbolic re-enactment of the meal of the Kingdom represents and releases the fullness of God in His nature and power to the world, in the same manner that Abraham modeled the Father's giving of the Son through his offering of Isaac.

The language of fathers and sons, I believe, is crucial for our analysis of the relationships we ought to cultivate around the Lord's kingdom banquet. If the Melchizedek blessing consecrated the fatherhood of nations and made Abraham illustrate the relationship between the Father and the Son through his life, what exactly is this model of spiritual parenting and divine sonship that we ought to emulate as members of the family of God? I believe it's not the same to consume a wafer at a religious gathering handed out by a professional minister as it is to partake as sons in relationship with our spiritual fathers, to exalt together in the Eucharist the eternal relationship of love that exists between the Father and the Son. We ought to grow in the community of our fellowship table as true sons of the house of God, eventually maturing to become future fathers in the faith.

> *"I am writing to you, little children, because your sins are forgiven on account of his name. I am writing to you, fathers, because you know him who is from the beginning. I am writing to you, young people, because you have conquered the evil one. I write to you, children, because you know the Father. I write to you, fathers, because you know him who is from the beginning. I write to you, young people, because you are strong and the word of God abides in you, and you have overcome the evil one." (1 John 2:12-14 NRSV)*

Apparently within the church it was established very early on that spiritual development was supposed to flourish within the context of becoming a spiritual family, with relationships defined between fathers and sons. We start as children, and by the love and nourishment of spiritual fathers, we grow strong in the word until we become spiritual parents ourselves. From the moment we are introduced as children to the forgiveness of sins through the process of blossoming in the Word to become seasoned in the faith, we are supposed to be nurtured in the vision of Christ's unity practice at the Lord's banquet. The mission is to release fathers speaking into the lives of their children, to see them assimilate the divine nature of the Heavenly Father.

> *"Do not speak harshly to an older man, but speak to him as to a father, to younger men as brothers, to older women as mothers, to younger women as sisters—with absolute purity." (1 Timothy 5:1-2 NRSV)*

If we would approach our worship gatherings as family reunions, seeing ourselves as extensions of the Lord's vision for communion, then the Lord's fellowship table would be honored, revealing our true identities to each other within God's community.

## Fathers Administering New Creation

Remember how we described Luke coloring the transfiguration as the dramatic illustration of the hidden potential of the Eucharist? We paralleled Emmaus with the mountain, seeing how on both occasions the Lord led his disciples to see all salvation history as reaching a climax of consummation at the cross, and how that redemptive work was mysteriously memorialized at the Lord's Supper. The kingdom was witnessed in the transfigured body of Jesus on the mountain, and that same body is now accessible in the transfigured elements experienced on Emmaus. The entire record of the mountain of transfiguration not only depicts the glory that is now available for the disciples in the sacramental presence of Christ, it also models the means by which that glory is supposed to be administered on Earth. Notice the pattern recorded in the scriptures; on the bottom of the mountain we see a father and a son struggling in their relationship. On the top of the mountain, we see the celebration of perfect unity and eternal union between the Father and the Son. What is the link between the glory above and the dysfunction beneath? It is the spiritual parenting and sonship of disciples being led up and down the mountain. The transfigured glory of the body of Christ is supposed to be administered by spiritual sons, learning the proper parenting of discipleship by the example of the loving relationship between the heavenly Father and the eternal Son of God. The Lord led them up the mountain, showing them the kingdom transfigured in His body, then memorialized His body in sacrament training, giving them how to transfer that glory down the mountain to the world. If there is any question that the fathers and sons theme is central to the discussion of the transfiguration, notice how the story invokes the motif of the ministry of Elijah, who is prophesied to restore the hearts of fathers towards the sons and turn the hearts of sons towards the fathers.

> *"Behold, I will send you Elijah the prophet before the great and terrible day of the Lord comes. And he shall turn and reconcile the hearts of the [estranged] fathers to the [ungodly] children, and the hearts of the [rebellious] children to [the piety of] their fathers [a reconciliation produced by repentance of the ungodly], lest I come and smite the land with a curse. (Malachi 4:5-6 AMPC)*

> *"Behold, I send My messenger, and he shall prepare the way before Me. And the Lord [the Messiah], Whom you seek, will suddenly come to His temple; the Messenger of the covenant, Whom you desire, behold, He shall come, says the Lord of hosts. (Malachi 3:1 AMPC)*

> *"And his disciples asked him, saying, Why then say the scribes that Elijah must first come? And he answered and said, Elijah indeed cometh, and shall restore all things: but I say unto you, that Elijah is come already, and they knew him not, but did unto him whatsoever they would. Even so shall the Son of man also suffer of them. Then understood the disciples that he spake unto them of John the Baptist." (Matthew 17:10-13 ASV)*

*"For all the prophets and the law prophesied until John. And if ye are willing to receive it, this is Elijah, that is to come." (Matthew 11:13-14 ASV)*

*"And he shall go before his face in the spirit and power of Elijah, to turn the hearts of the fathers to the children, and the disobedient to walk in the wisdom of the just; to make ready for the Lord a people prepared for him." (Luke 1:17 ASV)*

## Restoration of Fatherhood and Sonship

According to these scriptures, what prepares the way of the Lord for the establishment of the covenant is the spirit and power of Elijah bringing restoration of the fathers-and-sons relationship. The meaning of this restoration is graphically displayed on the mountain of transfiguration, where the alignment of heaven and earth is seen through the picture of proper spiritual parenting and the perfecting of sonship. There are three levels of these divine relationships, illustrated on the top of the mountain with the Heavenly Father and the sons of God, on the bottom of the mountain with natural fathers in connection with their flesh-and-blood children, and lastly in the journey up and down the mountain with spiritual sons learning the fatherhood of God through spiritual leadership. If we want to ascend to the glorious, transfigured nature of Christ, knowing the Father intimately as sons of the Kingdom, we must be equipped by spiritual fathers that model that relationship for us. If we intend to descend into the traumatized world of our confused generation, to confront the dumb and deaf spirits, we must go with the empowerment of the mountaintop experience, healing the broken-hearted with authentic spiritual parenting. What the disciples are learning in their journey up the mountain is the power of the Kingdom of God. They saw how that glory was manifested in Jesus' transfigured body, and that transfigured body is meant to bring restoration between fathers and sons. The transfiguration was introduced by this prophetic promise, inferring that the prophecy was about to be fulfilled in the mountain experience.

*"But I tell you of a truth, There are some of them that stand here, who shall in no wise taste of death, till they see the kingdom of God." (Luke 9:27 ASV)*

*"Verily I say unto you, There are some of them that stand here, who shall in no wise taste of death, till they see the Son of Man coming in his kingdom." (Matthew 16:28 ASV)*

There is confirmation in Peter of the fulfillment of this prophecy, showing that the correct interpretation of the experience is the foreshadowing of the coming of Christ.

*"For we did not follow cunningly devised fables, when we made known unto you the power and coming of our Lord Jesus Christ, but we were eyewitnesses of his majesty. For he received from God the Father honor and glory, when there was borne such a voice to him by the Majestic Glory, This is my beloved Son, in whom I am well pleased: and this voice we ourselves heard borne out of heaven, when we were with him in the holy mount." (2 Peter 1:16–18 ASV)*

Jesus himself foretold the disciples that they were about to witness the second coming, and then He was transfigured on the mountain before them, as if to show them how they didn't have to wait until the end of the age to experience the glory of the kingdom because that blessed state was already available in His sacramental presence. Jesus was training his future spiritual leaders for what His Kingdom is all about; the transfigured body is designed to lead spiritual sons into proper alignment with the Heavenly Father, and from that deep intimacy and communion descend into the world to restore the lost relationship between fathers and sons.

How do we father sons sacramentally? We lead them to the cross, teaching them about denying themselves and immersing them in the complete narrative of the Biblical story being consummated in Christ. That is the work of true discipleship: to teach leaders to be committed to the vision of community that delivers our generation from the dumb and deaf spirits that are destroying our spiritual and natural families. Let's think about ways we can become spiritual fathers, to train a generation of spiritual sons into complete transformation for the Kingdom of God.

> *"For though ye have ten thousand tutors in Christ, yet have ye not many fathers; for in Christ Jesus I begat you through the gospel."*
> *(1 Corinthians 4:15 ASV)*

Teaching about Christ and the sacramental life is not the same as living it to impart to others. Instructors can teach what they know, but fathers reproduce who they are. We have raised a generation that loves to listen to practical advice and principles to apply at their convenience, but their hearts are indifferent towards spiritual accountability and responsibility towards others. When we fill heads with instructions detached from relationships, that knowledge puffs many up into pride. Fathers share the experience of their lives to awaken hearts to the path of transformation that is to be followed in the presence of God. The goal is not only to succeed personally, but grow as faithful and loyal members of the body of Christ. The burden of fathers goes beyond the sharing of a lecture; spiritual parents live with the concerns of their family on their minds as a vocation. The vision of fathers is to model before their sons total conformity to Christ, to inspire those connected to reflect more of God's image in their lives.

### Fathers ought to represent accessibility to God before their sons.

When connected to our Heavenly Father, we enjoy the privilege of accessing His presence. That means belonging to His family, being welcome to inquire of Him without any hindrances. When we open our lives to others with that example of acceptance, it makes healthy discipleship grow into the connections that develop strong spiritual accountability. Making ourselves accessible to spiritual sons means allowing them to reach our hearts with their needs, struggles, and desires for deeper connection.

*Fathers ought to model before sons the responsibilities of being entrusted with the mysteries of God.*

That means the opportunities for managing sacred things together create awareness of the level of trust invested in the relationship. Often, we only understand fathers when we are placed in their shoes. By clearly communicating our intentions to our spiritual sons that we want them to be extensions of our heart and vision, we provoke them to seek greater understanding of our philosophy of life and ministry. Perhaps the reason why many disciples have not expanded beyond their current limitations is that they have never been given the opportunity to serve more as sons in ministry with their fathers.

*Fathers ought to offer to sons the possibility of enjoying true spiritual fulfillment.*

When a disciple can see and experience for themselves the beauty and depth of the life that is being offered in Christ, that brings the greatest sense of accomplishment in the life of true leadership. If sons never desire to reproduce the grace that was passed unto them and become isolated in their own opinions, seeking to find a life outside the Christ-centered community, that brings pain and sorrow to the heart of a spiritual father. One of the greatest challenges of leadership is to help disciples find joy and delight in learning how to love and be loved by others. The challenging conversations about marriage, relationships, parenting kids, and emotional and physical health are the subjects fathers ought to pursue with their sons to train them into a more fulfilled and meaningful spiritual journey.

## *The Heart of True Spiritual Parenting*

Of course, in order for any of these dynamics to work, there must be mutual collaboration. There's got to be a willing leadership and a receptive discipleship; if not, frustration and disappointment will cause a bigger gap to separate our generations. That is why the spirit and power of Elijah is invoked in the transfiguration story. Elijah transferred to Elisha a double portion of his spirit; the inheritance of the firstborn was delegated to him. The curse that separated the younger from the elder generation was broken, and the deaf and dumb spirit that causes sons to not hear or speak to their fathers was expelled. Elisha cried, "My father, my father!" He had become a true spiritual son, who sees, acts, and lives as his spiritual mentor. That power needs to come back to Earth, and there is no other place where sons and daughters of the Kingdom are shaped into spiritual connectivity to their fathers than around the fellowship table of the Lord. That is where the cloud of intimacy surrounds the voice of the Father over the transfigured body, and all of history finds a climax of resolution in the cross, consuming as sons in perfect union with the Father. Here are some ways we can ensure our communities are being built with the vision of authentic spiritual leadership for sons and daughters who are interested in shaping their relationships for the meal of the Kingdom.

**1. A real relationship between father and son should always be personal and intimate, knowing each other's hearts in order to truly operate in the same mindset.**

> *"But I hope in the Lord Jesus to send Timothy shortly unto you, that I also may be of good comfort, when I know your state. For I have no man likeminded, who will care truly for your state. For they all seek their own, not the things of Jesus Christ. But ye know the proof of him, that, as a child serveth a father, so he served with me in furtherance of the gospel." (Philippians 2:19-22 ASV)*

Paul is displaying Timothy as an example for others to contemplate and imitate. This means there is a strategic deliberation in presenting Timothy as a son, and not just a messenger or representative of his ministry. Paul intends that those under his care and influence approach their relationship with him from the specific mindset and posture of spiritual parenting. The emphasis of sonship is highlighted when Paul insinuates that those who don't operate with this disposition are looking for their own interest, not Christ's. Those are strong words; he is basically implying that people working in the ministry without the desire of being born spiritually as sons are not yet interested in genuinely serving Christ, but are still thinking only in themselves. So Paul is literally exposing Timothy to become a target of attacks and suspicions. Nevertheless, Paul is confident in what he knows of his son in the faith, and what Timothy learned from him. In order for the apostle to reach that level of trust, he had to pour a lot of time and energy into getting to know the innermost reflections of his disciple. In the same manner, he had to allow his spiritual son to see and understand the depths of his heart and love for Christ and his people. To think along the same patterns of ideas and embrace an identical philosophy of life requires a profound personal connection only obtainable by a serious commitment to a strong relationship. Sometimes we are not able to enjoy that level of transparency and vulnerability with many, yet that doesn't mean we should not entertain the desire of reaching that degree of communion with someone. Often, when I pursue a connection with someone interested in serving alongside me in the body of Christ, I open myself emotionally, sharing some of my feelings concerning my life and work. That means communicating to them my love for the people, sharing how much it hurts to see others suffer and close themselves to God. When someone is ready to be truly connected, they would probably assimilate those emotions and thoughts, and open themselves to experiencing them too. If they reject that burden of love, they would get emotionally distant and avoid sharing those sentiments with you. Getting to know people is hard work; some are professional pretenders and won't allow you to see their true intentions, conflicts, issues, and inner battles. Yet if we are fathers at heart, we must persist in challenging those around us to become spiritual sons, growing together with us as a family around the Lord's table.

**2. Fathers and sons must share a connection in the bond of the Spirit, partaking of the same supernatural process of maturity through the communion of prayer and impartation in the word of God.**

*"As ye know how we dealt with each one of you, as a father with his own children, exhorting you, and encouraging you, and*

*testifying, to the end that ye should walk worthily of God, who
calleth you into his own kingdom and glory. And for this cause we
also thank God without ceasing, that, when ye received from us
the word of the message, even the word of God, ye accepted it not
as the word of men, but, as it is in truth, the word of God, which
also worketh in you that believe." (1 Thessalonians 2:11-13 ASV)*

This is a very important and sometimes overlooked insight of spiritual parenting; our interactions with sons must be, first and foremost, rooted and grounded in our common experience of the presence of God. Some would learn your words, thoughts, and philosophy, but won't assimilate your heart, humility, brokenness, and passion. They struggle to take your words as from God because they don't have the same experience with God that you have cultivated. This could be a difficult scenario to explain, yet with spiritual discernment, you will be able to recognize when someone knows your doctrine but doesn't have your same spirit. That is, with some prospective sons you won't be able to identify the key characteristics of your intimate relationship with God, only a superficial understanding of what it produces in others. The word is not working for them because they don't use the word in their own personal walk with God. We must be self-aware enough to recognize what is predominantly in us to reproduce in others. Some are strong in the gift of intercession, others are fluent in the gifts of prophecy, and there are leaders whose most consistent grace is loving people, understanding them, and deeply caring for their wellbeing. Whatever is in you from God, be it intense worship, revelation of the scriptures, or a strong burden for evangelism, your spiritual sons should share that same spiritual DNA if they truly receive your words as from God, and not born out of the mere intellect of men. We are not called to create clones; every child of God is unique, yet God gave us a word that imparts and begets our particular fruit of Christlikeness in others. I believe that when we partake of the Lord's Supper together as sons of the kingdom, the experience of God we share in His presence will intensify to better comprehend what has been given to us through our spiritual connections.

**3. A true father genuinely desires the spiritual growth of his sons, and is actively seeking for the protection and well-being of those under his care.**

> *"My little children, of whom I am again in travail until Christ be formed in you—" (Galatians 4:19 ASV)*

> *"I write not these things to shame you, but to admonish you as my beloved children. For though ye have ten thousand tutors in Christ, yet have ye not many fathers; for in Christ Jesus I begat you through the gospel. I beseech you therefore, be ye imitators of me. For this cause have I sent unto you Timothy, who is my beloved and faithful child in the Lord, who shall put you in remembrance of my ways which are in Christ, even as I teach everywhere in every church." (1 Corinthians 4:14–17 ASV)*

We should keep our lives surrounded with responsible leadership: the ones who, by the inspiration of the scriptures and the power of the Spirit, are empowered by God to speak into our lives direction, vocation, and transformation. We all need examples of sacrifice, maturity, and consecration to God. We usually like to say, keep your eyes off man and look only to Jesus, yet Paul said, follow me as I follow Christ (1 Corinthians 11:1). The scripture also says to examine the example of your leadership and imitate their faith (Hebrews 13:7).

We too often like to say things that sound spiritual but are not scriptural at all; we attack leadership, criticize vision, and downplay the role of those who God Himself has placed in leadership to equip us and develop our full character and potential in the Lord. One of the curious developments of these texts is the importance of our connection to leadership. Paul speaks of those connected to him as if they are dependent on his travails for their character formation. He attributes to himself the responsibility of begetting them through the word, and he emphasizes that the key to their growth lies in the ability to keep following his example. Fathers should have a vision for their sons, and part of the future they should desire for those connected to them is to see them excel in their personal walk with God. Correction, discipline, and rebuke are not to be taken harshly when the sons know that everything that is done is implemented for the well-being of our souls.

**4. Fathers live sacrificing all they have, including themselves, for the sake of their sons. A true father is not interested in being compensated, and would never take advantage of the faith, love, and possessions of his sons.**

> *"Now I am coming to you for the third time, and I will not be a burden to you. I don't want what you have—I want you. After all, children don't provide for their parents. Rather, parents provide for their children. I will gladly spend myself and all I have for you, even though it seems that the more I love you, the less you love me." (2 Corinthians 12:14-15 NLT)*

As I write these words, my hope is that this message is not viewed as overly idealistic or unrealistic. In my own journey exercising many of these principles, the process has been very painful and troublesome. If not for intense prayer and constant remembrance of the Lord's Supper, my heart would have become hardened. The invitation to the table to be fathers and sons of the kingdom is a sharing in Christ's burden of love for His church. Sadly, today there is a complete abandonment of the theology of suffering inside our churches. We have neglected the importance of coming to the Lord's Supper understanding; we partake of His pains, struggles, and rejections in order to enjoy His grace to fulfill His mission.

> *"From now on, let no one cause me trouble, for I bear on my body the marks of Jesus." (Galatians 6:17)*

It is sad that many would reject the very thought of it. But when I am asked, what exactly is the work of a pastor, leader, and minister, my answer is: ministry is simply suffering. Of course, if you treat your vision as a career, run your church as a business, and pursue the success of ministry with the marketing ambition of today's Christian consumerism, you won't have a clue what I'm talking about. But for those who truly desire to partake of the real nature and burden of the Lord, those who desire to encounter intimacy in the knowledge of who God is in His presence and power, what you are asking for in ministry is nothing less than to share in the very sufferings of Christ.

> *"I am glad when I suffer for you in my body, for I am participating in the sufferings of Christ that continue for his body, the church." (Colossians 1:24)*

When you live your life by the example of Christ's love and sacrifice, no one will be able to understand your pain, especially when you pour your soul into empty vessels that do not desire for themselves the wellness that you desperately long for their lives to achieve. There will be no words for you to describe to others the agony and concern that will consume your soul as you pray day and night for broken marriages, rebellious teens, and wounded hearts who are dying, lost, and hurting without God. You will be granted the rare privilege to assimilate within your own being the unlimited and overwhelming love of God, but along with that joy comes the brokenness, desperation, and torment of experiencing how hurt, wounded, and rejected the heart of God is for humanity. You will ache, seeing the holiness of God insulted; you will crumble at the sight of the presence of God being disregarded and dishonored through carnality and indifference. You will die a thousand deaths in prayer, and carry upon your shoulders the afflictions and troubles of all those whom you love and care to see well. You will even feel the very assault of hell upon your whole being, coming with evil and darkness that will try to overtake your emotions, thoughts, and conscience with great spiritual warfare. There will be no one to call, no one to talk to, and the saddest of all will be when those who you have helped the most betray you, criticizing and mocking all that you have done for the Lord. In the midst of all that chaos, you will grow to see the glory and beauty of the wisdom of God. Even through the loneliness, you won't be totally alone. There will be a great awareness in the realization that only through all of your tears can your eyes begin to truly see the profound depth of love that God has for us all (2 Corinthians 1:3-7). In other words, there was no other way around it; only through partaking of these sufferings can our minds assimilate the worth, value, and revelation of the true message of the cross of Christ.

The cross is at the center of the universe, and it is the ultimate revelation of God for humanity, because in it we can see clearly without misunderstanding where God stands in relation to the world. That day when God Himself tasted of death in the person of Jesus of Nazareth, the weight of sin, the penalty of iniquity, and the cruelty of all evil fell upon a single individual who was completely consecrated in his passionate vocation towards God. There at the cross, the deep and lonely cry of love was heard in sorrow from the heart of Jesus, pleading for mercy, crying for forgiveness, and agonizing in perplexity with the tormenting question: "Why, God? Why have you forsaken me?" Who can answer that question when God Himself in His pain is the one doing the asking? At this level of intercession, answers are not what is required—empathy, assimilation, and union with God is what is called for. What we need today is more assimilators of the Lord's nature, and more intercessors that desire to partake of the pains and burdens of becoming one with God in prayer

We often preach revival, yet we neither understand nor intimately know the only one who can revive and awaken our souls. We have gone so far as to worship our own worship without knowing fully what or who we are supposed to be worshiping. The passion of God, the brokenness of prayer, and the solitude of intimacy are a foreign language for most Christian movements today who claim new awakenings and visitations from God. Where is the willingness to deny our own interest and the commitment to renounce our rights? Where is the dedication to forsake all and sacrifice ourselves for the cause of Christ? Where is the struggle against evil and fight for righteousness? Where is the cry for justice and the longing for truth? Where is the godly remorse over our sins and the pleading for the restoration of our purity and consecration for God? Today, we want the kingdom without the cross, and the benefits of relationship without the responsibility of loyalty. We want Christ's resurrection power without the conformity to His death. We desire to share in His love, but we want nothing to do with His sufferings. The early Church endured horrible tortures and suffered despicable deaths, paying the ultimate price for their faith. They had no problem undergoing such persecution, because they understood the privilege of sharing in the imitation of Christ's life, death, and resurrection. Their legacy should leave us a powerful example that encourages us to live lives as true witnesses for Christ. Instead of always looking for ever-increasing luxury and comfort, how about we start praying more scriptural prayers like that of Paul?

> *"That I may know him, and the power of his resurrection, and the fellowship of his sufferings, being made conformable unto his death." (Philippians 3:10)*

> *"Always bearing about in the body the dying of the Lord Jesus, that the life also of Jesus might be made manifest in our body. For we which live are always delivered unto death for Jesus' sake, that the life also of Jesus might be made manifest in our mortal flesh. So then death worketh in us, but life in you." (2 Corinthians 4:10)*

> *"But I will rejoice even if I lose my life, pouring it out like a liquid offering to God, just like your faithful service is an offering to God. And I want all of you to share that joy. Yes, you should rejoice, and I will share your joy." (Philippians 2:17)*

## Kingly Priesthood Reigning in Worship

There has always seemed to be a certain challenge for different Christian traditions to maintain a healthy relationship between word and sacraments, sharing the community life with believers and implementing the proper devotional rituals for authentic worship. Incorporating these various elements together in a responsible manner is the enormous burden of the institutional church and its leadership. There are interesting parallels between these struggles in the modern models of conventional worship and the established formats of Old Testament liturgical orders. Notice, for example, how the more traditional churches (Catholic, Orthodox, Coptic) reflect a greater interest in the reverential approach to God, featuring characteristics similar to those found in the tabernacle of Moses such as intercession, censers, vestments, priesthood, and rituals. On the other hand, the evangelical Protestant movements (Reform, Anglicans, Charismatics) adopt a style of worship that is more reminiscent of the devotion found in David's tabernacle, with prophesies, music, prayers, and spontaneous singing. There seems to be greater appreciation and respect in traditional forms of worship for the sacredness of space and the consecration of matter, time, and people in special moments and activities. In evangelical circles, the emphasis appears to be on personal responses to God: the proclamation and activation of the word by the witness of individual lives. That is not to say there is no reverence or holiness in Protestant churches, or that traditional congregations don't involve emotional or personal experiences for spiritual growth. But I find curious that traditional church members are less inclined to oppose leadership or usurp spiritual authority, while contemporary church communities are not as likely to close themselves into isolation to avoid being known personally. The churches adopting the David model of spirituality appear to relate more openly to personal convergence, while those embracing the Moses style of community reflect an affinity for more established theological stances. There was a time in Israel's history that David's tent and Moses' tabernacle coexisted simultaneously.[92] Perhaps that is a prophetic picture for us today, as both expressions of devotion are instructive in our Christian faith. It doesn't seem coincidental that the Lord's Supper is for the most part overlooked or not emphasized in evangelical circles, while it remains central within Orthodox forms of Christianity. It's almost as if the excitement of having the ark (the presence of God) like David blinds us from the serious vocational responsibility of living for God's glory (life of intercession) like Moses. These two prototypical systems don't need to be in opposition to one another; we probably should learn from both

---

92 1 Chronicles 16:37-40.

expressions of worship to incorporate them together in our celebration of the sacrament of communion. One doesn't need to become dispassionate or sterile because of being steadfast and rigorous in holding a spiritual discipline. And being personally awakened to a dynamic relationship with God doesn't need to become a self-absorbed idolatry used only for private spirituality. Maybe that's why David moved the ark back to Jerusalem, bringing forth a new revolutionary approach to the faith of the nation; he incorporated Moses' sacrificial system and his own spontaneous expressions of inspirational worship. His vision of building a unique house for the Lord (Solomon's temple) appears to be the attempt to bring heaven and earth together prophetically as a sign of the future Kingdom of God on Earth.[93] The king of Israel looks to be adopting the universal prototype of Melchizedek's priesthood.[94] He is becoming a king priest that intercedes for all people and seeks the restoration of all nations to the God of Israel.[95]

> *"On that day I will raise up the booth of David that is fallen, and repair its breaches, and raise up its ruins, and rebuild it as in the days of old; in order that they may possess the remnant of Edom and all the nations who are called by my name, says the Lord who does this." (Amos 9:11-12 NRSV)*

> *"Then a throne shall be established in steadfast love in the tent of David, and on it shall sit in faithfulness a ruler who seeks justice and is swift to do what is right." (Isaiah 16:5 NRSV)*

When David desires to build a special house for the Lord, he could be wisely recognizing that the Melquizedek order of priesthood not only preceded the Levitical order but will eventually supersede it.[96] He recognizes the value of the revelation of the tabernacle of Moses, so he

---

[93] Isaiah 16:5, Isaiah 22:22.
[94] 1 Samuel 23:9-12, 1 Samuel 30:7-8, 2 Samuel 6:14-15, 1 Chronicles 16:2.
[95] Acts 15:14-18.
[96] Psalms 110:1-7.

incorporates all its spiritual principles.[97] The temple of Solomon, which was given by revelation to David, was dedicated on the feast of tabernacles, which is also known as the feast of ingathering or harvest.[98] This specific feast was associated with the Messianic age and the restoration of the nations.[99] The temple David designed foreshadowed the reign of the Messiah on Earth for all peoples of the world. This house implemented all the holiness of Moses' rituals, and also the dynamic revelations of the tabernacle of David.[100] The vision for this place of meeting goes beyond the immediate location of Jerusalem; it is appointed for all cultures to come from all nations and see the glory of the Lord as a witness for future generations.[101]

> *"Likewise when a foreigner, who is not of your people Israel, comes from a distant land because of your name—for they shall hear of your great name, your mighty hand, and your outstretched arm—when a foreigner comes and prays toward this house, then hear in heaven your dwelling place, and do according to all that the foreigner calls to you, so that all the peoples of the earth may know your name and fear you, as do your people Israel, and so that they may know that your name has been invoked on this house that I have built." (1 Kings 8:41-43 NRSV)*

Could it be that the scriptures have provided the blueprint for our Kingdom worship as royal priesthood through David's vision for a temple? David, like Melchizedek, is a King and a Priest.

---

[97] 1 Chronicles 28:11-19. 9

[98] Exodus 34:22, Leviticus 23:42-43, 1 Kings 8:2, 2 Chronicles 7:8, 10.

[99] Zechariah 14:16, Numbers 29:12-34. Seventy bulls offered in the feast to represent the seventy nations of Genesis 10-11.

[100] 1 Chronicles 25:1-7, 1 Chronicles 6:31-32, 1 Chronicles 23:5, 1 Chronicles 23:24-32, 12.

[101] The place where the temple was built was believed to be the area where Abraham offered Isaac, and where the Messiah would eventually be sacrificed (1 Chronicles 21:18-26).

> *"Furthermore, the Lord declares that he will make a house for you—a dynasty of kings! For when you die and are buried with your ancestors, I will raise up one of your descendants, your own offspring, and I will make his kingdom strong. He is the one who will build a house—a temple—for my name. And I will secure his royal throne forever." (2 Samuel 7:11-13 NLT)*

The ultimate son of David was not Solomon, but Jesus, and the eternal house of the Lord was not the temple of Jerusalem but the body of the Messiah. What Solomon's temple foreshadows is the reign of peace of the Kingdom, intertwining different styles and formats of worship. Imagine if our celebrations of the Lord's Supper would honor the Lord's body and His blood of the new covenant, integrating solemn rituals coupled with divine inspiration, reverently presenting ourselves through liturgy and priesthood with the personal witness of our lives in word and deed. The Melchizedek priesthood was seen in David's life because he respected the laws of the tabernacle system enough to implement them in new, creative ways. After the king brings the ark to Jerusalem, he performs sacrifices. He rejoices, dancing before the Lord, and he blesses the people in the name of the Lord, sharing with them the components of a meal that seems to resemble Melchizedek's blessing.

> *"So they brought the ark of God, and set it in the midst of the tent that David had pitched for it: and they offered burnt sacrifices and peace offerings before God. And when David had made an end of offering the burnt offerings and the peace offerings, he blessed the people in the name of the Lord. And he dealt to every one of Israel, both man and woman, to every one a loaf of bread, and a good piece of flesh, and a flagon of wine." (1 Chronicles 16:1-3 KJVA)*

## Learning Systems for Our Present Devotion from the Past

What are some of the principles learned in the fusion of Moses and David's protocols of devotion? How we can adopt these insights into a more effective communication of the Lord's Supper for our lives today?

**1. Intercessory worship.** Having a collective conscience being represented by someone in the presence of God is not an idea to be forgotten in the Old Testament tabernacle. Moses' prayer to make the face of the Lord shine over God's people was a practice that trained the congregation to anticipate the same experience and glory that was upon Moses to also rest upon them. What one man assimilates in the glory, others can share in the same measure if they learn together to think and live as one entity before the Lord. One of the ideas we can incorporate from Moses' example is to allow leadership to express before God the words that in agreement represent the sentiment of the congregation. When general prayers are done, benedictions are made, and rituals are conducted, we should visualize ourselves as being part of those formalities. This mindset should not be limited to rituals or liturgy; we should be able to identify with each other in our experiences and testimonies. One of the fascinating novelties of David was allowing others to contribute their talents, gifts, and creativity in their service before the ark. Now the people not only can see themselves through a representative, they can connect to each other and transfer their unique experiences to others in the presence of the Lord.[102] That model of David's vision for worship, combined with Moses' mediatory system, shows us the possibilities that can be explored in the corporate gatherings of believers when we unite as the body of Christ.

> *"For as the body is one, and hath many members and all the members of that one body, being many, are one body: so also is Christ.*
>
> *And whether one member suffers, all the members suffer with it; or one member be honored, all the members rejoice with it. Now ye are the body of Christ, and members in particular." (1 Corinthians 12:12, 26-27 KJVA)*

If a leader understands the needs of the body, he should be able to address the complexities of the congregation in an articulate manner, using the light of the scriptures so that people can hear their hearts

---

[102]1 Corinthians 14:26, 14.

being unveiled through intimate conversations in the presence of God. When people together identify with what leaders are saying on their behalf, suddenly they can better comprehend their own hearts' issues before God. Those celebrating the Eucharist should boldly represent God's people, expressing before the Lord their pains, joys, confusions, and desires, and also receiving passionately in their hearts the answer for all to enjoy at the moment of the celebration of communion.[103]

**2. Organized awakenings.** The appreciation for structure, order, and spiritual discipline seems to be lost in many Christian communities. The tabernacles of Moses and David were both about constant routines, not just dependent on a sudden outburst of spontaneity. If a format has proven to be providential for divine visitations, there is no need to sacrifice on the altar of innovation. The songs of the Lord's birth during musical services in David's tent were often unrehearsed and unplanned, but the appointment of the ministers and their assigned duties were all scheduled and organized. Routines are important to strengthen values, preserve traditions, and cement essential convictions for our spiritual development. When David got too carried away by his creativity, he sought to incorporate a cart that was reminiscent of the Philistines' handling of the ark of the covenant. It's almost as if he attempted to copy the grace that was upon the Philistines' rituals, presupposing that since they got away with that novelty, perhaps Israel would too.[104] The lesson learned was that vision for opening the presence of God to everyone is not the same as opening everyone's system to the presence of God. When Uzzah touched the ark and tried to help, he was judged by God and stricken dead at the spot. There was already an established protocol, a proven method by which to handle the ark; it was upon the shoulders of consecrated Levites. David wanted the ark in Jerusalem, but he needed to incorporate God's proven formalities in the process of transferring the presence of God. The art of remembrance honored in the tabernacle of Moses was established by the persistence

---

[103]Acts 27:21-26, 30-36. If interpreted sacramentally, this text would mean Paul interceded on behalf of all those on the ship, and was granted through his intercession the salvation of their lives, something he celebrated by the breaking of bread.
[104]1 Samuel 6:7-8, 2 Samuel 6:3, 6-7.

of rituals commemorated in repetition. Continually refreshing our souls is going to require that, like in the tabernacle, we cultivate true spiritual habits. From morning to night, there was a daily format to follow, and a weekly one also. The schedule was not supposed to be altered, and around the year there were specific feasts to be celebrated at appointed times and seasons revolving around the temple. If today we desire revival for our churches, we must ask ourselves how strategic we are concerning our treatment of the Lord's Supper. I don't mean simply how often we are keeping up with our monthly communion services, but in a broader sense. In what practical ways are we creating relational habits for regularly endorsing Christ's vision for community, giving ourselves in sacrificial love and imitating the example of Jesus to serve others? Is there a place for the Lord's table in our hearts? Do we honor it in our homes by our daily routines? How prepared are we for communion when we celebrate it at our churches? Moses' legacy was all about training the mind for the sanctity of space, time, and matter; David's vision was all about opening the heart to continually enjoy intimacy with God in His presence. We can have both dynamics at our communion services, but more importantly, we need to implement them regularly at our daily walk with God.

# 9

# Living the Sacramental Life

Do we see any patterns in the scriptures of how the vision of communion practically shaped the early lives of the believers? How is the message of being the body of Christ and living in consecration under the blood of the new covenant relevant to the structure of our ministries and churches today? The book of Acts is probably the best blueprint, and our best sample of the bread and wine of Jesus in action in the New Testament. It is often forgotten that this book is actually the continuation of the first volume of Luke, which described the life of God that was seen in Christ. With that thought in mind, we can see how Luke is hinting throughout Acts that the life of God that was seen in Christ is now operating in a sacramental way through His church. The church is the body of Christ, continuing Jesus' mission and passion, and expressing His divine life as a new living organism for God's vision on earth. The Christ that was incognito as Mary's baby, and later disguised at the Emmaus road with the disciples, is now tabernacle in a new shape and form within His assembly of believers, who are living the sacramental life by faith. Let's see an example of how the divine life of God operated inside the early church to display the vision of Christ to the world. There is no character that has affected the formation of the church more than the apostle Paul. Luke, in the book of Acts, chronicles his conversion, but more importantly, he articulates a pattern that models the church's implementation of Jesus' principles of the sacramental life in a practical way.

## *Stephen*

The first step in the divine encounters of Paul with the body of Christ is seen in the life of a believer named Stephen. Saul of Tarsus is said to have overseen his execution, yet something curious is described at his death. Stephen prays and interceded for his attackers, and says:

> *"As they stoned him, Stephen prayed, 'Lord Jesus, receive my spirit.' He fell to his knees, shouting, 'Lord, don't charge them with this sin!' And with that, he died." (Acts of the Apostles 7:59-60 NLT)*

When was the last time you heard those very same words before?

> *"Jesus said, 'Father, forgive them, for they don't know what they are doing.'*
>
> *Then Jesus shouted, 'Father, I entrust my spirit into your hands!' And with those words he breathed his last." (Luke 23:34, 46 NLT)*

Do you see how Luke is portraying the life of God that was in Christ now operating in the sacramental life of the church? Stephen is emulating the cross, and the principles of forgiveness learned at the breaking of the bread. For him, the table was not just a ritual, it was his lifestyle. The importance of this account is that it shows the power of the symbolic act behind the death of this martyr. We can assume that his self-emptying humility and forgiving attitude had a lasting effect on his chief persecutor, Saul of Tarsus. Luke is careful to tell us that all this was done in the service of the conversion of Paul.

> *"...and dragged him out of the city and began to stone him. His accusers took off their coats and laid them at the feet of a young man named Saul." (Acts of the Apostles 7:58 NLT)*

The book of Acts is showing us a blueprint for spiritual awakening and Kingdom expansion. This divine life, when properly applied in

Christ-centered fashion, will have the power to birth the apostle Paul, who represents in this context the transformative, revolutionary move of God for our generation. At the time of this event, many were aware that the church was at a crossroads in defining its identity to the world. That Christianity might disappear just as another Jewish sect was a real threat. The clarity to ensure the survival and preservation of the body of Christ, doctrinally and culturally, came as a result of Paul's conversion. Therefore, the sacrifice of Stephen's death was not just an unfortunate casualty of history. It was, in a sense, an emulation of the atoning death of the Messiah for the impartation of divine transformation. The stoning of Stephen became a pivotal turning point in the history of Christianity and humanity as a whole, because Paul, the catalyst for change, was produced as a result of the example of the faith of this martyr. Curiously, on a small side note, the name "Stephen" means "crown." Crowns regularly speak about authority, dominion, and kingship. Could it be that this whole narrative is concealing the mystery of how the breaking of the bread operates within the true Christian community to secretly manifest the Kingdom of God on Earth? I believe this could very well be the case. If Paul, the representative of the move of God, was born in this crowning moment through the living Christ operating inside the church, what principles can we learn from the sacramental life of the body of Christ?

**Jesus did not come to be served, he came to serve others.**

One of the most moving scenes in the gospel narratives is Jesus' washing of the disciples' feet. The Lord is humbling himself by doing an action that was assigned to slaves. He is cleaning the feet of people that were about to deny him, and were arguing about who would be the greatest amongst themselves. How sharply these different philosophies of service contrast! While the disciples sought the advantage of reputation over others, Jesus chose the esteeming of others above himself. When we come to the vision of attending to those who are members of the body of Christ, we should emulate the self-deprecating posture of Jesus. The Kingdom meal is about pursuing the needs of others, and not only focusing on our own needs for validation and recognition. The followers of the Messiah have the challenge of constantly illustrating humility without allowing it to be confused for weakness. To express confidence that does not cross over into arrogance produces the kind of responsible leadership that is always sensitive, accessible, and honorable. Members of the body should model by example the culture of transparency that doesn't sacrifice respect.

When Stephen comes to face his execution, he resembles the example of the Son of God by being willing to lay it all down in service of God's glory. Stephen is, in a sense, washing Saul's feet with his own life and blood, as an intercessory prayer to birth him into the very body he is persecuting and seeking to destroy. The image of the clothes of Stephen laid at Saul's feet is very moving. The blood of this martyr is demonstrating to the future apostle the evidence of another way of doing life and showing devotion towards God. What a challenge, when attacked, criticized, or persecuted, to choose to offer up prayers and extend forgiveness! The way of the cross is to recite the words of Jesus: "Father, forgive them, and let my sufferings serve as a means for their reconciliation." We live in a society where people feel entitled to have everyone serve their needs while not being willing to supply the needs of God's kingdom. One of the things I most despise in the Christian culture is the viewing of others as utilities, or means to an end. I have heard this perspective advertised in different ways in various leadership circles. People say things like, "If the people you are with do not help you to get to your next level, get rid of them." I always wonder: what exactly is this next level we are trying to get at, where people are no longer important unless they serve our own carnal and selfish interests? The sacramental life is not about viewing the body and blood of the Messiah as disposable items to serve one's own convenience, it is about imitating the example of the Lord carrying our cross of sacrifice for the well-being and benefit of others.

**Jesus did not come on the Earth to live, but he came to die.**

> *"He that findeth his life shall lose it: and he that loseth his life for my sake shall find it." (Matthew 10:39 KJV)*

This is indeed a revolutionary statement. I think there is more to it than what may appear on the surface. Paul the apostle said something that reminds me of this word of Jesus:

*"Yea, and if I be offered upon the sacrifice and service of your faith, I joy, and rejoice with you all." (Philippians 2:17 KJV)*

*"As for me, my life has already been poured out as an offering to God. The time of my death is near." (2 Timothy 4:6 NLT)*

The image of pouring ourselves out empty upon God's vision, investing our energy, time, and resources to promote the heart of God for His people: that is the way to be truly fulfilled in our lives. This is not a mentality of seeking to get as much out of everyone and everything as we can; instead, it is about being willing to lose everything we possess for a cause worth dying for. We will find true joy, satisfaction, and self-realization when we let God's passion consume us for His heavenly ideals. The Lord showed us an example of not pursuing his own interest, not taking advantage of his rights, denying himself, putting others above himself. When Stephen was not concerned for his own self-interest, but only fixing his gaze upon pursuing the glory of God, his eyes were open and He could see the Kingdom.

*"But Stephen, full of the Holy Spirit, gazed steadily into heaven and saw the glory of God, and he saw Jesus standing in the place of honor at God's right hand. And he told them, 'Look, I see the heavens opened and the Son of Man standing in the place of honor at God's right hand!'" (Acts of the Apostles 7:55-56 NLT)*

One can say this evangelist found his life. There is a phrase used to describe reckless living: "burning the candle at both ends." Some use it as a figure of speech, to refer to being all used up or wasting one's life. I would like to redeem that phrase in the context of the sacramental life. If we are eating and drinking of the life of a man that, with possession of full divinity, let His life be burned up completely for our sake, we should allow that sentiment to overtake us and fuel us to do the same for him.

**Jesus did not come to impress, but to express the nature of God.**

The church has too often become a center of entertainment instead of a house for transformation. How much of our faith would remain if we stripped from it all the things done based on performing for appearances? Stephen had nothing to show off. He was simply being faithful to a clear vision of surrender and abandonment, in imitation of the life of Christ. To stand alongside a minority view and boldly proclaim the convictions of something truthful was the only objective of this evangelist. Our modern perspectives on spirituality are so tainted by the illusion of growth and success that we may not even recognize authentic faith and devotion to God. How many today would risk their lives for a small Passover meal alongside the persecuted revolutionary, rather than the massive popular feast of the priests celebrated in the illustrious temple in Jerusalem? The truth is that the glamor and glitter of belonging to something with status and influence (meaning the temple) is more attractive than the challenge of sacrificing reputation and comfort to follow someone who promises the hope for a better future (Jesus). What we represent in values sometimes is more important than what we produce in accomplishments. Stephen may not have achieved things people interpret as valuable or successful, but he expressed something pure, faithful, and transformative. Having a lifestyle that revolves around the Lord's Supper means to think, act, and speak symbolically in everything we do. The motive, inspiration, and convictions being lived are more important than the results being achieved. The nature of God is love, and everything we do must be with that focus. Nothing we communicate should be contaminated with self-seeking objectives or distorted motives. Look at this curious text:

> *"If I gave everything I have to the poor and even sacrificed my body, I could boast about it; but if I didn't love others, I would have gained nothing." (1 Corinthians 13:3 NLT)*

How can anyone sacrifice their own life for others and yet have no love? Our altruism could very easily be born out of the deceptive lust for hero worship. There is also the martyr's syndrome, someone pretending to suffer for others only to get attention or pity for their own pain. Sometimes it's harder for us to live for God than it is to give ourselves in sacrifice, dying for Him. Therefore, our suffering cannot be a coping mechanism for escapism, cowardice, or deliverance from guilt; these mechanisms could readily become a real danger in our spiritual quest for genuine expression of the love of God. Our motives and incentives are just as important as our values, character, and behavior. Even in suffering, the cause promoted, the image represented, and the vision endorsed must always be in alignment with God's divine nature. Although Jesus' calling was to serve others and give His life as a ransom for many (Mark 10:45), the *way* he did it was just as important as *what* he did. Christ could not make a spectacle out of his own vocation, throwing Himself down from the pinnacle of the temple (Matthew 4:5-6); neither could He allow others to cast Him down by force just because he loved them (Luke 4:28). These were all false imitations of His real and ultimate call of dying on the cross for humanity, in the perfect revelation of the love of God. It could not be done by external force, nor by an internal Messianic complex, but only out of obedience to His God-given vocation. Only as an extension of the overflow of God's love in His heart can he truly say, "No one takes my life, I lay it down voluntarily of my own accord" (John 10:18).

If love, even in an ultimate sacrifice, is so tricky, how can we learn to love like Jesus loved (John 13:34)? The answer is that we must learn to live like Jesus lived. Two specific ways come to mind:

- Jesus lived the cross-shaped life of discipleship. Obedience is better than sacrifice, but that does not mean that obeying is not sacrificial. Self-denial and total surrender to God's Spirit is the best expression of a true, loving sacrifice. Our modern versions of the gospel constantly seek to advance our own agendas, looking for the exaltation of our best interest and pursuing the massaging of the flesh instead of its crucifixion. When we yield in consecration to our discipleship, God will give us His divine nature, showing us how to truly love not in our own strength, but according to His divine power.

- Jesus lived the lifestyle of intercessory prayer. The best gift I can offer the people I love is to pray for them, because God can love them in ways that my limited mind does not understand. When I lay down through intercession my own carnality, selfishness, and personal ambition, I not only release the will of God for those I pray for, I ascertain the heart of God for them, loving them with God's perfect love. Prayer is not just the vehicle to change things; it is also the primary tool God uses to transform us to learn to love others the same way He loves us.

## *Ananias*

Luke is not done with Stephen, who shows us the mysteries of the sacramental life of God that was in Christ now flowing through His Church. Paul was impacted by the divine encounter of the risen Lord that appeared on the road to Damascus. Yet he was blinded and confused, having no ability to understand what his next course of action should be. His world had been turned upside down, and he was helpless to know what to make out of it all. Think about our previous discussions and meditate with me on how tragic this situation really was for Paul. The next move of God was birthed, supernaturally conceived, yet there was no hope for it to be fully developed and released into the world. This is the very condition of many churches, ministries, leaders, and new converts within Christendom. If we don't possess a community meal, where the nurturing aspects of God are transferred into the lives and visions of individuals, we will continue to cyclically miscarriage God's purposes. The very New Testament, the Gentile church, and the spreading of the gospel over the entire known world was inside a man who no one wanted to mentor because everyone was afraid of him. Notice that only people full of the essence of the life of Christ could accept the challenge to tenderly forgive past offenses, seeing beyond the present condition of undeveloped potential. The Paul experiment needed healing and reconciliation, growing within the secure environment of God's loving grace. If Christ is not properly communicated to this vessel of revival, he will grow twisted and become spiritually unfruitful. He needs someone to open his eyes to a new way of thinking, living, and believing. He needs to see Jesus through the corporate body of the Messiah to assimilate the true nature of God, awakening his gifts and receiving him as a full member of the family. From Stephen, Paul goes on to encounter Ananias. Do you know what the name "Ananias" means? "YHWH has been gracious." There are some very powerful words spoken by Ananias to Paul that must have felt deeply moving and liberating:

> *"So Ananias went and found Saul. He laid his hands on him and said, 'Brother Saul, the Lord Jesus, who appeared to you on the road, has sent me so that you might regain your sight and be filled with the Holy Spirit.' Instantly something like scales fell from Saul's eyes, and he regained his sight. Then he got up and was baptized." (Acts of the Apostles 9:17–18 NLT)*

The shining face of Stephen, now the loving embrace of Ananias; this is what Paul needs to apprehend the complete revelation of the body of the Messiah, working in concert to manifest the glory of God in the face of Jesus Christ. Ananias knew the terrible things that Saul of Tarsus had done. But he also knew the power of the atoning blood of Christ, which changes lives and restores fallen human beings back to their allotted destiny. *People afraid of dirt will never experience the joy of unearthing treasures.* Hearing the words "brother Saul" coming from the representative of the church he had just persecuted probably brought deliverance to the apostle Paul's soul and heart. He was not just welcomed to the household of faith with open arms, he was appreciated and supported to ensure his progress. The fellowship table of the Lord, when it is lived in practice, will extend grace, forgiveness, and nourishment to all those who are born within the family of God. The healthy environment where the image of God can shape the divine reflection of the full life of the Son of God is only ascertained through communion.

What are some of the principles of the sacramental life of Christ that were demonstrated through the example of Ananias' life? How can these principles inform us today on how to nourish and bring about God's destiny for our generation?

**Jesus did not come to intimidate through fear, but to set us free by His love.**

I believe our God is hidden within every human relationship we encounter in life. But often, we fail to recognize the beauty, power, and truth of such reality, especially when we abuse and neglect the communion and fellowship with those who are close to us. The truth is, the distance between us and God is easily reflected in the distance we create with those around us. The more intimacy we experience with God, the more openness we are supposed to encounter with those God appoints to our life. Therefore, segregation and isolation can only mean spiritual perversion. Paul allowed Ananias to become the Christ figure he needed to assimilate in human form. He received the embrace of a stranger as if it was the Lord Himself. Notice how God is already revealing Himself to Paul through the reality of the humanity of Ananias.

> *"I have shown him a vision of a man named Ananias coming in and laying hands on him so he can see again." (Acts of the Apostles 9:12 NLT)*

God wants Paul to assimilate the reality of His loving hands by the means of a new personal relationship. The sacramental life is all about allowing the body of Christ to become the immediate experience of Jesus for you. To allow someone to become special to you in that manner is a choice and a conscious effort, and it requires our receptiveness and vulnerability. The apostle John said:

> *"We proclaim to you the one who existed from the beginning, whom we have heard and seen. We saw him with our own eyes and touched him with our own hands. He is the Word of life. This one who is life itself was revealed to us, and we have seen him. And now we testify and proclaim to you that he is the one*

*who is eternal life. He was with the Father, and then he was revealed to us. We proclaim to you what we ourselves have actually seen and heard so that you may have fellowship with us. And our fellowship is with the Father and with his Son, Jesus Christ. We are writing these things so that you may fully share our joy." (1 John 1:1-4 NLT)*

This verse could very easily go overlooked and unappreciated. Notice how the apostle is exhorting people to come in close proximity and fellowship with each other so they can experience the very same communion they encounter when they walk with Christ on Earth. This is almost like saying that the incarnation has not ceased. Jesus is still accessible, with the same quality of His nature of love available through new human vessels: divine embodiments of the life of God.

**Jesus did not come to have selective mercy, but to exemplify unselfish compassion.**

Too often, we seem to only be concerned or do good for those who can do something in return for us. If that is our interpretation of our communion meal, Paul would never have been invited to be a part of our fellowship gatherings. I want to bring into account an Old Testament example of what I believe is the true sacramental life of Christ. I am referring to the selfless act of love of Jonathan for David. Jonathan loved David, even while that meant having his own father turn against him. Jonathan was the rightful heir to the throne, yet he renounced his rights, position, and personal gain for the sake of seeing his friend take over the kingdom over which he was supposed to reign. We are often good at loving those who can help us get to where we want to go. How about loving and serving the ones who are anointed by God to take our place? At one period in time, David, Saul, and Jonathan sat together to eat at the same dinner table; there was so much potential, power, and glory at that family meal. Yet it all ended in tragedy. Can we ever learn how to grow covenant relationships, honoring, respecting, and remaining loyal to one another—even when our own personal interest suffers? Probably only if we get a true revelation of the sacramental life of Christ in action. Jesus, while on Earth, focused on helping, reaching, and advancing the cause of the neglected, forgotten, and rejected. His table was filled with those who had no reputation or credentials. For the church, Paul represented the enemy, the threat to their survival. Ananias, by the revelation of the Lord, was able to see in Paul the future: the opportunity for change, and a witness of the true vision and power of God's kingdom.

**Jesus did not come to build programs, but to transform people to establish kingdom relationships.**

One of the most moving aspects of the gospel story is how Jesus prayed for the selection of His twelve apostles. He selected a group of people and committed himself to their lives, through all the ups and downs, the struggles and storms of life. He changed their identity, and prophesied into each one of them their true value in regards to their purpose and future together in the kingdom. He never gave them false expectations, and always bluntly stated the challenges and dangers of following His vision. Jesus not only trained them, he delegated responsibilities and tasks to get involved in God's vision. The Lord was very specific in His treatment and dealings with each one in his inner circle. By having such close association and investment in who they were as people, he gave them a blueprint to follow as to how to enjoy life together. There is a lot we can learn from Jesus' reliability in the Holy Spirit's work, within and amongst His disciples. Jesus knew what His disciples would experience inside them in the fullness of the Spirit when they connected to God wholeheartedly. They would know the future, and they would be guided into truths. They would be reminded of His words and teachings with greater insight. They would have greater intimacy and understanding of Jesus' person, work, and vision. There would be a greater ability to deal with the internal affairs of men's hearts. All this is important to understand when looking at the sacramental life. We are not working alone when we are building a Christ-centered ministry; the Holy Spirit is alongside us to shape our unity and perfect our relationships. It is not possible to build Kingdom culture without having some sort of involvement in people's lives in order to release that Holy Spirit dimension in their hearts. There was profound, deep work of the Holy Spirit in regards to Paul's past sins, convictions, and doctrinal presuppositions.

The Lord was revealing a man with the name Ananias praying, caring, and being gracious unto him. I believe in a sense that spiritual introduction was important to later be able to handle his social interactions with this divinely appointed man of God sent into his life.

## Barnabas

We are seeing the layout that Luke designed in the book of Acts to show us the operation of the kingdom of God, which is different for all the systems and structures of the world. When believers are committed to the vision of communion becoming the body of the Messiah, miracles, signs, and wonders are released on the Earth. The Lord's Supper was not just a dogma to be kept in liturgy, it was a principle of life that informed and inspired all their words, deeds, and thoughts to express the glory of Christ in a tangible, practical way—starting with what we label as the birth of the transformative move of God, represented in the life of the apostle Paul. This is followed by what we identify as the nurturing of God's future, illustrated by the receiving of sight of Saul of Tarsus done by the prayer of Ananias. Now we come to a third phase of progression, described by Luke in the promoting and endorsing of Paul to be acknowledged officially by the authority of the church. Paul has been born and nurtured through the intercession of Stephen and the discipleship of Ananias. But his full potential and scope of influence has not yet been unleashed. For the most part, we can say Paul remains in the periphery with regards to the full range of his possible impact on the world. He is still largely unknown, and viewed with uneasiness and reluctance. No one seems really sure about how to evaluate his significance. He appears to be in need of some sort of recommendation or approval that could settle his spiritual status once and for all. That is when our next Christ-type character comes onto the scene, to express yet another dimension of the sacramental life of Christ.

His name is Barnabas, which means "the son of encouragement." This man apparently had good standing, solid reputation, and wide influence in the Jerusalem church. He used all his credibility and spiritual equity to sponsor Paul into wider recognition. Whatever we birth and nurture on Earth will never reach greater heights of prominence if we are not willing to adopt this principle of Christlikeness modeled in Barnabas' life. How far and wide will our effectiveness in the world be? I suggest it will only reach as far as the parameters of Christ's life in us will allow. Jesus stood at the table to gaze at a group of disciples with the promise of having greater works for them to do. Why? Because he was going to use His standing and position before the Father to manifest wider spheres of grace and power through their lives. The ultimate endowment from heaven that will show us the fullness of God on Earth will be completely seen when we learn how to actively pursue the advancement of the life of Christ in others. Barnabas recognized the gift of insight and the transparent authenticity of the life of Christ in Paul. He saw the relevance and value of Paul's ministry being advertised for the advancement of the kingdom to a larger audience. Paul could not, and cannot, do it on his own. He needs someone who knows how to raise others onto higher platforms. This truth is vital for the unlocking of the sacramental life. Everything we possess at the table is entrusted to us for the sake of releasing others into greater heights of kingdom blessing. What practical principles do we see in the example of Barnabas that we can apply to our search for the sacramental life?

**Jesus did not come to have a local vision, but to raise a global movement.**

There are ideas that many won't even consider when it comes to elevating the vision of Christ's body to a wider audience. Things like using our favor to position others to succeed, as well as advancing fresh and relevant ideas through new vehicles and channels of accessibility. Barnabas was a bridge, a promoter of others. It seemed that he had an eye for the hidden potential of others and recognized how far they could spiritually reach. Jesus possessed that quality in His divine life. While he was on Earth, the Lord truly raised the faith of his close followers to greater heights. His aspirations for the expansion and influence of his disciples can be witnessed when He said to them statements like: "Greater works than these you shall do." This ambitious principle of the life of God in Christ, seen in Barnabas, can look like an impossible task for many of us who live within small faith communities. But perhaps we should not be easily discouraged by the monumental challenge of thinking globally. Instead, let us pursue greater connectivity with the impact God is already having beyond our own spheres of influence. The obvious, easy start to that adjustment of thinking is modifying our prayers. The world has become smaller within our generation due to the prominence of social media. We can now more than ever before be open to the needs of other people. The spiritual and social climate of different regions and nations is no longer unknowable. The sacramental life is celebrated locally, but it is experienced universally by our spiritual connection to God's eternal church. The saints of all ages and the believers alive throughout the entire world are all presented spiritually at the fellowship table of the Lord. That vision should fill us with amazement and excitement to play our role in communicating God's message to a global stage. Barnabas catapulted Paul towards a wider platform. I wonder what depth we could find in others if we started unlocking the life of Christ hidden inside all those who have been assigned to our lives.

Have you ever noticed how many times a person who has a profound and relevant message does not necessarily have the tools or platform to disseminate their information to their targeted audience? Isn't it strange how many people who control large spheres of influence and management often lack the message or vision to effectively maximize their resources in a productive manner? Why would someone have to abandon the urgency and potency of their insights to try to pursue the reputation and recognition of a valid venue for their voice? Many prefer to hold on to the oversight of their platform, even if their message is empty of substance, than to share it with someone unknown who would take advantage of the social and cultural assets they possess. No wonder we are stuck locally in our mentality, fighting over limited social real state. Jesus always had in mind that His fellowship table would be a place to transfer His spiritual riches and divine empowerment for a worldwide awakening.

*"And this gospel of the kingdom will be preached in the whole world as a testimony to all nations, and then the end will come."* *(Matthew 24:14)*

*"Truly I tell you, wherever this gospel is preached throughout the world, what she has done will also be told, in memory of her."* *(Matthew 26:13)*

Previously unrecognized, marginalized, and ostracized people now have a place at the table to share their testimonies and experiences. Like Barnabas, those who can use their status and prominence to discern truths inside unknown vessels can gracefully magnify these unique messages to reach greater spheres of impact to the masses. Jesus basically said in the great commission to go into all the world and repeat what he did—to live sacramentally because his table has the power to reach all dimensions and structures of life. Barnabas was one of those who expressed the divine life toward the apostle Paul, causing the spiritual revolution that was inside Saul of Tarsus to expand and permeate not only all of the known world but all generations afterward. Barnabas was a facilitator who illustrated to us the importance of using our gifts, tools, and favor to enlarge God's kingdom. The world will not be reached if we don't learn how to surrender our platforms for the service and well-being of Christ's body, even if it costs us our personal preferences and aspirations. Maybe the reason we currently possess a certain degree of spiritual revenue and cultural leverage is to promote a vision greater than ourselves. If Paul truly represents in the book of Acts the hidden potential of the Body of Christ when the sacramental life is lived in unity, then Luke is depicting for us what the church could accomplish if we restore the blueprint of having true communion inside every one of our corporate communities. The visitation of heaven will impregnate our being, like it did Stephen, conceiving the move of God that later birthed the apostle Paul to the nations. Like Ananias, we will develop the discipleship of healthy apostolic ministry like the one that nurtured the New Testament Church, and finally, we will expand our territory, maximizing our gifts, resources, and talents. As exemplified through Barnabas, we will take the unknown into notoriety and the unexpected into prominence by releasing true revival on the earth.

**Jesus did not come to gather followers but to release leaders.**

Beyond the barrier of reaching multiple disciples, we face the challenge of raising a legacy of faithful leadership. If we could create a habitat for the development of apostles, prophets, teachers, evangelists, and pastors, perhaps then we can build a new spiritual community that unites ministries, families and churches with limitless capacity and boundless capabilities. Often, we only view the releasing of leaders in the context of sending people oversees like missionaries or sending people on a special assignment to help other ministries. Yet Jesus' way of enabling his future apostles to unleash their spiritual endowment was to create opportunities for them to exercise their faith, collaborating with Him in the grace of God that was over his life.

But how can we do that? Perhaps we need a change in perspective, philosophy, and attitude towards our leadership skills, goals, and agendas. Let's ask ourselves a few questions. If God is developing a world changer within our congregation, would we be able to identify their specific ministry potential, or would we end up being intimidated by their leadership qualities and skills, suppressing their efforts and initiatives? If a person joins our team for an extended period of time, would they feel compelled to remain faithful to our vision or will they eventually grow distant from our heart, drawn away gradually by the superficial approach we have to our church's system? Are people within our sphere of influence attracted to our spiritual passion? Are they willing to sacrifice and follow our example of consecration or are they indifferent, distant, and clueless to what God has placed inside of our hearts? The example of Barnabas illustrated in the book of Acts shows us how a deep connection of partnership can release effective collaboration in ministry when done with mutual respect and appreciation. The apostle Paul found in Barnabas the type of leadership that encouraged exponential growth and enhanced unique vocational opportunities. The same strategy and vision that was demonstrated with Christ's leadership continued through the book of Acts with characters that learned how to unlock the wealth of spiritual riches residing inside the hearts of others. I am fascinated how in Jesus' humanity his heart was always seeking for those around him to operate in the same realm of effectiveness that He enjoyed in His relationship with God. When Peter wanted to walk on the water, Jesus did not say, "Are you crazy! Don't you know who I am? How dare you ask me permission to partake of something that took an entire life of consecration to master?" Instead, the Lord basically said to Peter, "I like your attitude. Come walk with me!" Then suddenly, someone who was not at the same level of communion with God as Jesus, began to operate in the same level of grace that was upon Him. Barnabas speaks to us about Christ's divine attribute of unbinding and unraveling the constraints to our proficiency. When no one believed in Paul and everyone on the Jerusalem council was afraid of him, Barnabas, who was full of the sacramental life of Christ, fought to introduce him at the table of leadership to sit alongside the other apostles. Once Paul tasted that level of grace and experienced that sphere of authority in his life, he excelled in his oversight and began walking on the water. The seed alone without the right environment will not germinate the ultimate harvest. We as sacramental people are responsible for creating the same atmosphere for growth that Jesus had for his disciples. When we approach the Eucharist, that is a moment of solemnity when we should ask God to fill us with the divine nature that causes others to flourish in grace and maturity. If I were preaching a sermon on these essential principles, I would title it: Don't drop it! From Stephen to Ananias to Barnabas, Luke is carefully articulating in Acts how Paul was the direct result of the sacramental life of Christ. When the church insisted in gathering followers in Jerusalem, it sparked persecution upon believers, but when the body of Christ scattered, releasing leadership into the world, everything hidden in the life of Christ began to manifest the Kingdom!

**Jesus did not plan to stay, he strategized to leave.**

The legacy of the Lord can be seen by the specific virtues and features that the church adopted such as the vision for chastity and purity amongst a promiscuous generation, the acts of compassion and philanthropy that benefited society even when they were unpopular, the insistence of proclaiming the good news by traveling and witnessing to others even in the midst of persecution, and the militant posture of moving against the influences of darkness to promote deliverance and transformation in spite of unprecedented resistance. Christianity emerged with the specific shape it undertook because of the unusual heritage of Jesus of Nazareth. None of these specific characteristics could have been preserved if not for Jesus' resolve of leaving a generational influence through his followers. When the Lord asked the disciples, "Who do you say that I am?", he was not only stimulating them to receive revelation from the Father as he did, he was also encouraging his future apostles to carry forward the mantle of mission assimilated through their direct experience of Christ. Jesus was inviting His followers to shape the course of history alongside Him with prophetic dialogue and providential conversations.

We are standing today in the 21st century as the benefactors of the momentous exchange of inspired thoughts shared between Jesus and Peter. The rock of foundation upon which Jesus will spiritually build His dream house on earth was being established through the speech of leadership who were trained to handle the responsibility of administrating the Lord's eternal legacy. None of our lives are long enough to fulfill everything the Kingdom meal of discipleship has to offer for this world. We have seen how by the model of the sacramental life, the corporate body of the Messiah was able to produce the ministry of Paul, a revolutionary movement that reached far beyond the time of the inauguration of the infant church. The composition of the New Testament documents, the discipline of what is known today as systematic theology, the merging of the gentile and Jewish believers into one body, the preservation of the Christian church through first century persecution, and the evangelization of the known world within one generation was all accomplished in the book of Acts because the power of sacraments was being practiced in life and not just known in theory. The church expanded as foretold by Jesus from Jerusalem to Judea, to the utter most parts of the world. But the means by which they infiltrated the world was turning enemies into converts, and murderers into apostles, inverting the very weapons that were meant to destroy them as instruments of breakthrough and blessings. The cross was shaping their communities with radical love, extravagant forgiveness, and sincere sacrifices. To be a part of the Lord's table, eating of God's atonement, was illuminating and empowering. They didn't just celebrate a mundane ordinance of eating food ritualistically. They partook of the preservation and impartation of the divine attributes that were idealized in Jesus' earthly life. When Paul says we are all together beholding as in a mirror the glory of the Lord and are being transformed into that same image, he literally witnessed that likeness in the face of all those who as the body of Christ molded him into maturity. Our community banquet is supposed to be all about going back to our true Christlike heritage to pass forward the legacy of the meal of the Kingdom. The Lord said to His disciples that it was expedient that he go away because from his glorified state, he can always be in every community meal to embody His divinity—birthing, nurturing, and raising greater heights for His corporate body. The sooner we debunk the myth of our own legend, the faster we will establish connections that ensure perpetuity for our true eternal legacy.

## Dining with the Enemy

The betrayal of Judas is often overlooked when describing the events that transpired in the last moments of Jesus' life. I think it is important to recognize that if we aspire to live the sacramental life, we must take into consideration the role of Judas at the table. Even when not highlighted, Judas is an example of one of the most influential and essential ministries getting overlooked and neglected in the development of the Christian life.

Jesus gave him the same bread he shared with the rest of the disciples. To our knowledge, Jesus kept the poisonous matter of Judas' flaws private, and loved him with the same grace and deference that he offered the others. The Lord never removed him from his responsibilities, regardless of his deficiencies. Many pastors would be fired from their positions if people found out they were treating staff members with that kind of philosophy of ministry. The sacramental life often will be confusing and challenging to the carnal mind unless we get the divine perspective of God on the role of the bread and wine in the life of a betrayer. Think with me for a moment; how do we know if we are truly repentant or remorseful for past behavior? Have we really forgiven our offenders and released them from their spiritual debts in our hearts? In what way can you be certain that your love and loyalty towards others is not simply based on social convenience or strategic, hidden selfishness? If we allowed those who apparently served no purpose to our interests to be received and loved with the bread of communion, then we could examine the depth of our motives and confirm the fruit of our authentic Christlikeness. When you decide to embrace the vision of the sacramental life of Jesus as your main priority, there will be great resistance and opposition to that commitment. The main attack against that vision will come from those who are close to you. It was not just Judas who walked away from Christ after communion, it was all of the disciples, including Peter their leader. But behind all the trials and tribulations, there is always a hidden purpose and divine conspiracy working for our spiritual growth.

Let's be honest, we often need help developing patience with others—especially when dealing with the purity of our true intentions in relationships. How else can we experience confirmation about the hidden motives of our hearts, other than being challenged in a close relationship with a traitor? Only with true purpose, commitment, and faith can anyone bear the hostility that comes from breaking bread with an adversary. If we desire our convictions to be grounded in total humility, then our loyalty needs to be tested with the friendship of those who seek to conspire against us. It is the pressure of loving the unlovable that forces our faith to have complete dependency on God. That alone maintains our focus in having the eternal destiny of God always present in our minds. If Christlikeness is the goal, then the drama of sitting at the table with an enemy is central and crucial for our spiritual development. I may not like the stubborn, but those close-minded people keep us humble; through them we understand that it is not our charisma or knowledge that changes hearts, but only the mercy of God. It doesn't matter how much I seek to avoid the difficult, rebellious, demonized opposition of carnal believers; they will always show up to draw me closer to God in prayer.

Remember, keep your friends close and your enemies closer. That was originally used as wisdom employed by the mafia in the *Godfather* movies, but we as believers can redeem the advice as wisdom applicable for our spiritual growth in Christlikeness.

## *The Judas in Us All*

There is a very real possibility that our proximity to the fellowship table of the Lord will be the very medium by which God exposes the forces that seek to destroy His purpose in and around us. When in communion, we evict demons from our hearts; then we provoke the exodus of the manipulative soul ties retreating from our lives. Faithful witness to God's goodness will always expose the hidden darkness in our humanity. I wonder how many secret conspirators are lying dormant within our spheres of influence because we have not properly unleashed God to reveal their true nature. All the disciples experienced this phenomenon of confrontation at the dinner table. I believe this was an unavoidable feature of their gatherings while they were eating together remembering the Lord. There will always be betrayals from within and all around us, but we must remain faithful, trusting that God has everything under control and will eventually even use the apostates for His own purpose and glory.

> *"While they were eating, he said, 'I tell you the truth, one of you will betray me.' Greatly distressed, each one asked in turn, 'Am I the one, Lord?' He replied, 'One of you who has just eaten from this bowl with me will betray me.'" (Matthew 26:21-23 NLT)*

I think the most practical application of learning from the betrayer is asking ourselves: Lord, is it I? In fear and trembling, our prayer perhaps should be, Lord, I don't want to be Judas, disinterested and disjointed from the communion, only thinking of what is in it for me—looking close to others on the surface, pretending to love the master with the kiss of hypocrisy, but with my heart indifferent and hardened by selfishness and pride.

## *The One Bread is a Complete Loaf*

One of the main lines running across this book has been the unity of the church. The act of celebrating the loaf of bread is, in its purest form,

a congregational event. Having someone connected to you who represents Christ is essential in understanding this remembrance. Living in
a communal setting that reminds you of Jesus' vision for a faith family
is crucial in order to assimilate the power of this sacred moment. One
of the neglected aspects of the unity of the church is our relationship to
those who have gone before us. The scripture says we are surrounded
by a great cloud of witnesses. The book of Hebrews declares we have
come to Mount Zion:

> *"No, you have come to Mount Zion, to the city of the living God,
> the heavenly Jerusalem, and to countless thousands of angels in a
> joyful gathering. You have come to the assembly of God's firstborn
> children, whose names are written in heaven. You have come to
> God himself, who is the judge over all things. You have come to the
> spirits of the righteous ones in heaven who have now been made
> perfect." (Hebrews 12:22-23 NLT)*

If there is a triumphant universal church in heaven whose purposes
are intertwined with our destiny here on Earth, shouldn't we want to
feel like a part of the vision of such a community? There should be
joy in the comprehension that we are part of something greater than
ourselves. There is continuity between past generations and ours. We
can assume that even future generations are intertwined with our
lives and work here on Earth when we prophetically leave a legacy for
them to follow. The scripture clearly attests to this spiritual connection, showing the different dynamics that provoke us to think with
a transcendent perspective when it comes to our unity with the body
of Christ. I believe reflecting upon those who have overcome death,
awaiting the final resurrection in the glorified body of the Messiah,
alleviates our anxieties about the ending of our natural lives. It is as if
we are getting a foretaste of our future glory when we see those who
are now alive in the presence of God. Jesus said that God is known
as the God of Abraham, Isaac, and Jacob, meaning he is surrounded
with those who he continually sustains in His presence as their God.
As we are caught up into experiences of glory, we sense how one day

we will be remembered on Earth. We are getting direct revelation of how the Holy Spirit is connecting all of our works, dreams, and longings together for his purpose, weaving them towards God's future. This exercise is part of our engagement with the broken body and the shared blood of the Messiah. At the Last Supper, Jesus was facing death, and by way of example he was instructing us on how to go through this dark season of our lives alongside him. Jesus, in his broken body, has made death to us what the cross became for him. The place with the worst evil darkness can offer becomes a medium to release God's healing and redemption. Contemplating our own mortality in view of the death and resurrection of Jesus gives us the correct attitude towards the sacramental life in general. We are living for one another in the present, because in eternity, that is all that will count for all those who are following the example of Christ. There is nothing to be afraid of, because perfect love has cast out fear.

> *"Because God's children are human beings—made of flesh and blood—the Son also became flesh and blood. For only as a human being could he die, and only by dying could he break the power of the devil, who had the power of death. Only in this way could he set free all who have lived their lives as slaves to the fear of dying."* *(Hebrews 2:14-15 NLT)*

What better way to show death its defeat than to acknowledge the great company of believers who, by being united to the resurrected Christ, are no longer controlled by its power? Many people have trouble finding the correct language or attitude to handle the struggles of losing a loved one. This is where the Lord's Supper provides a powerful image of communion with all those that are alive in the presence of God. When we are all united as one body, all the heavenly realities of the glorified body of the Messiah are open to us, including our anticipation of the final reunion with all the saints that are waiting for the manifestation of the Kingdom of God on Earth. I wonder, when we remember Jesus' life on Earth, how real to us is that Jesus that we recall by the scriptures? He is not here visibly, yet He is with us spiritually, perhaps even more deeply and intimately than with any of those people who only met his human body physically on Earth. In other words, knowing someone bodily is not the only way to experience them. You may say: "But Jesus is God! Of course we can encounter His reality spiritually." Well, think about John the Baptist coming in the spirit and power of Elijah. Apparently John was able to walk in the spiritual essence and divine grace that was on him many years after he was gone. We can mention also the mountain of transfiguration, where Moses and Elijah appear talking with Jesus. The book of Hebrews describes all the previous generations of the chosen people of God as if their lives on Earth are intertwined with ours. They were living on Earth with the purpose of leaving a spiritual inheritance for us. By the scriptures, we can partake of those spiritual mantles they left behind for us to apprehend the fruit of their testimonies by faith.[105] Even Paul the apostle mentioned the grace that was upon his life being transferred beyond the limitations of his physical body.

> "Even though I am not with you in person, I am with you in the Spirit. And as though I were there, I have already passed judgment on this man in the name of the Lord Jesus. You must call a meeting of the church. I will be present with you in spirit, and so will the power of our Lord Jesus." (1 Corinthians 5:3–4 NLT)

> "For though I be absent in the flesh, yet am I with you in the spirit, joying and beholding your order, and the steadfastness of your faith in Christ." (Colossians 2:5 KJV)

There are more dimensions to human beings than what we touch, see, and encounter in our physical proximity to people. That is why we can be surrounded by people and still feel all alone inside. Many of us only know people from an Earthly point of view; that is why they become disposable and useless once they leave this Earth.

---

[105]Hebrews 11:13, 39-40, 1 Corinthians 10:6, 11, 1 Peter 1:10-12.

> *"So we have stopped evaluating others from a human point of view. At one time we thought of Christ merely from a human point of view. How differently we know him now!" (2 Corinthians 5:16 NLT)*

Embodiment is central to becoming a person. Certainly, without corporal reality there is no point of reference or content for personhood. Yet that does not mean that embodied creatures can only exist or be truly known in their physical state. In fact, for many of us it has come as a surprise to find out that some of the people who spend the most time with us often are the very ones who know us least. There is another component to who we are that is known only to God and whoever God chooses to reveal it to. That side of us is the one that is available in the presence of God, not only to others but to ourselves. What a revolutionary thought— many of us will not even know ourselves properly unless we come to the revelation God has of us in the presence of the glorified body of Christ.

> *"Now we see things imperfectly, like puzzling reflections in a mirror, but then we will see everything with perfect clarity. All that I know now is partial and incomplete, but then I will know everything completely, just as God now knows me completely." (1 Corinthians 13:12 NLT)*

When we gather as the people of God, everything that is known to God about ourselves is supposed to be accessible in His sacramental presence. That is why we not only can come to grips with our own true identity, but also discover who others are supposed to be to us in God's providence. Here is another curious text to examine.

> *"If the dead will not be raised, what point is there in people being baptized for those who are dead? Why do it unless the dead will someday rise again?" (1 Corinthians 15:29 NLT)*

Baptism is about passing from death to life in the death and resurrection of the Messiah. How is involving dead people in this ritual significant to the matter of the discussion about resurrection? Many theories have been offered to answer this question. I don't seek to add more speculation to our current discussion. But whether it be that we are so connected as the body of Christ that people on Earth can take the place of a deceased person to perform baptism in their place, or be it that remembering saints was so important that people adopted their names on Earth as if to continue their legacy starting at baptism, one thing we cannot say is that people who pass away were just forgotten and viewed as unimportant in the sacramental practice of the early church. Resurrection meant that death is not the end to the relationships we enjoyed on Earth. Baptism meant somehow we are immersed into the body of a larger family than the ones who are alive on Earth. All those saints who are no longer with us are still a part of the same body, and that should be at the very least remembered as we celebrate the one bread, which is a complete loaf in the presence of God.[106]

## *The Memory of the Departed is Sacred*

Let us meditate on this interesting subject for a moment. Why do we see in human beings the phenomenon of honoring the memory of those who transitioned from this world? Why is it that we as a people feel as imperative the need to remember those who pass away with reverence? What is it about us that we cannot easily let go without first giving proper honor towards the memories of those who are no longer with us on Earth? My theory is we do all these ceremonial rituals because, deep down in our hearts, instinctively we know that the memory of those who pass away is sacred to God.[107] Think about how strong our instincts to honor the memory of a person that has passed away are, that we cannot speak of them the same way did while they were still alive.

---

[106]In all this discussion, I am not insinuating that one could or should seek to speak to the dead. Neither am I encouraging the practice of praying for lost loved ones. I am simply reflecting on the reality of heaven, and the assembly of believers that is present with us at the moment of the celebration of the glorified body of Christ.
[107]Psalms 116:15.

Now we say things like "may he rest in peace" or "bless his soul," etc. We even bring gifts and presents to their tombs, making beautiful memorials to visit regularly. How interesting it is that we feel strongly enough to behave in such a manner?

I have become convinced that our strong sense of reverent remembrance is not accidental; it is literally a spiritual exercise that we encounter when we are faced with the reality that the memory of those who have passed away has become sanctified by God as his own possession. In other words, at the very moment people disappear from this world, God makes their memory his own treasure, and from now on to think of them we have to deal somehow with the Lord first. If we want to contact all that the deceased person meant for us and others, only God has the power to release it. This is significant because we must learn that people always belonged to God, and in the last instance, they are His creatures made for his own pleasure and glory. People carry God's image on Earth, and they conceal His nature in all the things they express in their existence. God, almost like a loan or a spiritual lease, allows us to be stewards: administrators of our relationships, friendships, and companionships here on Earth. These hidden interactions inside people with God's image have the potential to release deep, intimate revelations of who God is for us. We perhaps must always remind ourselves that all that is meaningful, beautiful, and truthful about our relationships here on Earth is what God allowed to be expressed and experienced in our humanity. Without Him, none of those things could possibly be enjoyed.

For instance, when God wanted to show how He can be our brother, He gave us the gift of brotherhood. Because God is our Heavenly Father, He made sure we never forget that truth by giving us the image of unconditional love in our Earthly parents. God is a friend, so He gives us friendships; He is a husband so He gives us marriages. All these things are preparations of our eternal inheritance: knowing the depths of the love of God. God is always with us, in and through all the things he created. We just need to open our spiritual eyes and see Him revealing himself all around us. I have come to learn that even when we lose loved ones, God is still here with us in a very special way through our memories, thoughts, and prayers for those ordained by God to reveal something significant of who He is to us. Nothing God intended as a gift for us is lost forever in His presence. If we come to Him, we can still withdraw everything God hid of Himself in our lost loved ones from that well of revelation.

When we come to the fellowship table of the Lord, the one bread of which we partake is the complete universal body of Christ. All the saints from all generations admiring the complete, finished work of the resurrected Christ enjoy the victory of his glorified body. I believe the simple act of thinking about this amazing truth can change the way we approach the mysterious power of the Lord's Supper in our lives.

# 10

# The Culmination of the Bread and Wine

## *Communion in the Book of Revelations*

The perspective of communion as a celebration of judgment and consummation is conveyed graphically in the book of Revelation. This is not the first place many would imagine to find references to communion. Yet while not obvious at first glance, the whole vision of John the revelator ends in what the scripture describes as the marriage supper of the Lamb. The heavenly banquet that is commemorated and anticipated throughout all of church history is predicted to be fulfilled in Revelation 19:7-9, Revelation 21:1-6. It is the destination of the marriage between heaven and Earth. The entire consummation of God's salvific plan in the book of Revelation is seen as the result of the ministry of Jesus applying the eternal judgments of God from heaven, according to His priestly and redemptive work accomplished through the cross. In other words, the sacrifice of His body and the shedding of His blood qualified the Lamb to sit on the throne of glory and receive from the Father the eternal inheritance that contains the destiny and future of all creation. How does Jesus govern the entire order of the universe according to the book of Revelation? By the principle of his sacrificial death and the grace of the new covenant in His blood. The book opens with the vision of Jesus standing in the holy place dressed and adorned as the high priest of our faith. As the mediator, intercessor, and judge of all things, he rules over his assembly and executes his sovereign dominion over all creation. Jesus is pictured as coming out of the throne of glory. He is ministering from the heavenly holy of holies, ready to give out of Himself to the church what he shares in the nature of the Father.

In the book of Revelation, we see the heavenly vision of the authority of our high priest ministering with the power of his blood to exalt the virtues of the new covenant. Jesus is seen in this vision as the lamb of God seated on the throne of glory. From his exalted position, he is in control of all the sufferings, tribulations, and judgments that transpired throughout the world. Even all the evil, death, and hell itself is subject to his kingship. This is important because the way darkness appears on the Earth is not the ultimate truth of things. John the visionary is stating, "Look at the throne. The one who was killed is the one in charge of all creation, the one who was slain through his death has defeated all the evil in the world by his suffering." Jesus is ministering to his church from this divine perspective, making us share in his supernatural essence to reign on the Earth as kings and priests unto our God. Like Jesus, we exercise dominion, ruling with the mindset of his divine nature exemplified in his sacrifice. We imitate the Lord's worship, denying ourselves and giving ourselves over to God by the power of his blood. When the veil is opened and the heavens are exposed in the book of Revelation, then we see how the redemptive work of the Messiah is clarified. It may look like we are persecuted and forsaken, but in reality we are triumphantly entering into our eternal inheritance.

*"And they have defeated him by the blood of the Lamb and by their testimony. And they did not love their lives so much that they were afraid to die." (Revelation 12:11 NLT)*

Persecuted Christians could easily lose heart, believing in a King who cannot save them from the attacks on their faith. Yet John provides new lenses to transform the believers' ultimate worldview. In our kingdom sufferings are crowns of glory, and apparent defeat releases greater eternal praise unto our God, because Jesus, our example, uses the worst things this world has to offer to accomplish His providential plan and execute his judgments.

Let's see how in the opening chapters of the apocalypse, every one of the promises of the Lord to His church comes as an extension of who He is as the human and divine priest desiring to communicate to us the partaking of His glory. He is sending His Spirit, His angels, His word, and His glory from His throne, ministering to all the churches from His heavenly temple. Notice the promise to the church of Ephesus inviting them to the tree of life in God's paradise. We analyzed previously this motif of journeying back to the Garden in Chapter 2. We explained how the tabernacle was like a new Eden, training us to come back home to glory. This is similar to the reference to the crown of life we see in Revelation 2:8, telling the church in Smyrna they can be delivered from the second death—which is another reference to immortality. The descriptions of Jesus promising specific eternal things to his church are intended to evoke the world of covenant worship. The allusion to the hidden manna and the stones with new names at Pergamum is an easy echo of the miraculous bread in the holy of holies, only seen by the priests. The morning star at Thyatira is nothing less than Jesus himself, with all his authority and dominion, promising to give himself with all his influence to his body. Being clothed in white and having our names confessed before the Father and his angels, described to the church of Sardis, was exactly what the high priest did with the people of God inside the tent of meeting in the old covenant. Becoming a pillar in the temple, inhabiting and revealing the nature of God, describes the language of our eternal worship to the church of Philadelphia. All these things are said to be transferred from Jesus to us by His Spirit as we come into alignment with His heavenly virtues flowing from his heavenly temple. All these promises can be interpreted as sacramental in nature because they are a direct result of Jesus, as our high priest, offering himself in the heavens as our eternal offering and priestly representative. As explained before in previous chapters, if worship within the first churches was conducted around the format of a spiritual banquet, then the visions of John will serve as a spiritual sketch of what we are really enjoying in the heavenly realm as we partake of the kingdom meal.

> *"Look! I stand at the door and knock. If you hear my voice and open the door, I will come in, and we will share a meal together as friends. Those who are victorious will sit with me on my throne, just as I was victorious and sat with my Father on his throne."* (Revelation 3:20-21 NLT)

The risen Lord who walks among the seven candlesticks is speaking to his universal church. From his glorified state as the human and divine priest of all creation, he addresses all the evil in the world and inside His divine assembly. The visions of the book poetically describe Christ's position in the heavenly courts with the conditions inside each of the particular churches. For example, to the church of Ephesus, the one in the midst of the candlesticks warns about removing their church's candle. What is true of Christ in the heavens reveals what can potentially be true of us as part of His body on Earth. It is as if there is a heavenly counterpart to every earthly reality. If we allow our high priest to properly minister to us through his gifts and presence, we can reflect more of his image. The one who was dead and now is alive, the first and the last, warns of being faithful unto death to receive from him the crown of life. This he said to the church at Smyrna, as if saying that since he conquered death, all the people of God can therefore be victorious over death by persecution. If we receive his grace and empowerment flowing from heaven, there won't be any fear of losing our lives now that we have gained heavenly immortality. To the congregation of Pergamum, the Lord speaks as the one who has the double-edged sword in his mouth, implying he will give us the divine word to fight and make war with that very sword against all false teachings and doctrines that oppose his purposes inside his body. What a tremendous promise. We can spiritually fight with truth, with the same authority that is in our King, with the word of God.

The high priest of our faith is concerned with our spiritual condition. He is ministering on our behalf in the heavenly realms of glory.

By the power of His Spirit and through the agency of His messengers, he is confronting the darkness in and around us to bring new glory out of our lives unto our Father. In another example, Jesus is shown in Thyatira as the one having the eyes of fire, examining and searching the hearts and minds of the congregation to give to all people according to their deeds. This shows that it is the Lord himself who purifies his church and cleanses His people, so that we can all truly reflect more of his heart and character to the world. What would happen if we came before God's throne to be filled with everything available within our heavenly high priest? Imagine us walking into the inner courts of glory, receiving the influence of the fullness of the Spirit of God. Operating supernaturally with the key of David. Opening things no man can open and closing things no man can close. Entering into higher dimensions of worship in intimacy with God, and expressing heavenly melodies that bring the romance of heaven to Earth.

Every time we approach the celebration of the bread and wine of the kingdom, we are invoking the spiritual reality of this heavenly scene in the book of Revelation as we desire to connect to all of the majesty and splendor of our King. We are approaching the throne and proclaiming, along with all of the heavenly creatures, the triumph of the Lamb that was slain. The suffering of the Messiah, the blood of His covenant, and the excellence of His humanity have been accepted and enthroned in glory. We have that insight now in the presence of God; therefore, we are not troubled by the afflictions and tribulations of our earthly lives. In the sacraments, we are communing with our eternal inheritance and partaking of Christ's divinity by His grace. What is true of him will be true of us, as the veil is removed from our consciousness and we behold his glory in the bread and wine of the kingdom.

This imagery running throughout the narrative of John's vision is like a spiritual projector. These projections illuminate our imaginations with the beauty of the invisible realm that surrounds us during sacramental worship. Think about the power that is illustrated every time we lift the cup of blessing, with this specific blueprint in mind of the lamb that was slain sitting on the throne. Celestial beings and eternal creatures are perplexed at the profound connection between us and Christ in our liturgical worship. The confusions, inner conflicts, contradictions, and traumas of life are dissipated in the knowledge that everything harmful, destructive, and perverse is under the control of the Lamb of God. No matter what comes against us in this world, all things have already been defeated and conquered on the cross. Everything that is fallen, broken, and disjointed in creation is ultimately being used for God's redemptive purposes. That is what the scroll in the hands of the Lamb of God represents in Revelation 5. The sovereign Lord has all things under his administration and supervision, bringing every situation in this world into alignment with and subjection to His divine design.

*"Then I saw a Lamb that looked as if it had been slaughtered, but it was now standing between the throne and the four living beings and among the twenty-four elders. He had seven horns and seven eyes, which represent the sevenfold Spirit of God that is sent out into every part of the earth. He stepped forward and took the scroll from the right hand of the one sitting on the throne. And when he took the scroll, the four living beings and the twenty-four elders fell down before the Lamb. Each one had a harp, and they held gold bowls filled with incense, which are the prayers of God's people. And they sang a new song with these words: 'You are worthy to take the scroll and break its seals and open it. For you were slaughtered, and your blood has ransomed people for God from every tribe and language and people and nation. And you have caused them to become a Kingdom of priests for our God. And they will reign on the earth.' Then I looked again, and I heard the voices of thousands and millions of angels around the throne and of the living beings and the elders. And they sang in a mighty chorus: 'Worthy is the Lamb who was slaughtered—to receive power and riches and wisdom and strength and honor and glory and blessing.' And then I heard every creature in heaven and on earth and under the earth and in the sea. They sang: 'Blessing and honor and glory and power belong to the one sitting on the throne and to the Lamb forever and ever.' And the four living*

*beings said, 'Amen!' And the twenty-four elders fell down and worshiped the Lamb." (Revelation 5:6-14 NLT[108])*

## The Marriage Supper of the Lamb

All of human history is moving towards an apocalyptic event that the Bible calls the marriage supper of the lamb. On that day, the purposes of God for humanity will finally be fulfilled. What exactly is the ultimate desire of God for His creation? It is the joy and intimacy that comes from the union of entering into the eternal marital covenant with Him. Marriage is an interesting mystery. When we enter into this covenant with another person, in a sense we cease to be who we are and we become something altogether different, which must be discovered and experienced in our assimilation of our love for each other. In many ways, marriage is a way of unveiling our purest and truest hidden identity. As we have discussed before, we are currently in a stage of prophetic engagement with our heavenly bridegroom. Yet we already experienced the disclosure of intimacy with God that transforms us from glory to glory[109]. Do you remember the story of Jacob and his two wives, in which Jacob means to acquire his beloved Rachel but was tricked by Laban into marrying Leah, her sister? Why I am bringing this story to mind? Because marriage is shown in these passages as a revelation of all that was hidden inside Jacob's identity. Before Israel can come out of Jacob, he must confront and change everything that is buried deep within his soul. Just like Jacob was one of two brothers fighting for his father's affection, now Jacob is a husband of two sisters fighting over the acceptance of his love. Jacob is forced to look in the mirror of his soul and face his inability to be intimate and transparent in his relationships. He is ironically placed in the position of his father

---

[108]If we accept in the texts the references to the Lamb as echos of the Passover celebration consummated in the Eucharist then all power authority and dominion is being release through the church at the moment we join heaven to commemorate the Last Supper.

[109]2 Corinthians 3:17-18.

so that he can understand the difficulties of giving to others what does not come naturally out of ourselves. He is now supposed to give to Leah what he once longed for from his father and never received. Would he give what was not given to him? Can he redeem the personal offense of his father by loving Leah? Can he give affection out of knowing what should be expressed to someone that deserves to be loved? Yet how can Jacob love Leah when she reminds him of the deception of Laban, who tricked him into marrying her? Leah reminded Jacob not only of Laban's manipulation, but of his own deceptions when he tricked his brother Esau and father Isaac into receiving the inheritance. This story shows the difficulties of true intimacy. We are victims of our own past experiences, traumatized, unable to ascertain true union with God in worship. Marrying someone exposes the deep issues and deficiencies in our identities. God so loved us in Christ that He gave us a rite in our spiritual engagement to be healed from all our past wounds and failures. That is where the cup of blessing works on our behalf, revealing our true self in intimacy with Christ. The Lord, in our stage of betrothal, is purifying us to present us unto himself as a glorious bride.

*"...to make her holy and clean, washed by the cleansing of God's word. He did this to present her to himself as a glorious church without a spot or wrinkle or any other blemish. Instead, she will be holy and without fault." (Ephesians 5:26–27 NLT)*

We don't want to be like Jacob, marrying an illusion of someone that we don't truly know, because in reality we are not even in touch with our true selves. He slept with Leah all night thinking she was Rachel. I wonder: who exactly do we think Christ is when we approach him? If we don't allow his cup of communion to show us his true nature, how can we enter into true covenant worship? The cup of blessing is literally Christ preparing us for the future marriage supper of the Lamb.

One day we will all be together as one. Sincerity, honesty, and transparency will be the new norm, and the lies, hypocrisies, and deceptions about ourselves and others will end. We will look each other in the eyes with nothing to hide, finally free from guilt and shame. There we will have incredible and meaningful conversations, and we will at last be genuinely interested in what others want to say to us. We will open to each other the innermost parts of our hearts, and beauty, majesty, and joy will satisfy our every need as we commune in dialogue.

We won't worry about time anymore. There will no longer be fear about the future, our dreams, or our aspirations. Every desire, passion, and ambition will be realized and fulfilled without the tainting pollution of our self-serving motives. We will hope beyond all hope. We will fully trust without any reservations. We will radically love in extravagant intimacy and purity, and there in the midst of it, God will be the center of everything.

I don't just want to wait for that day to come. The greatness of the gospel is that we can begin to practice now in the power of the Spirit the habits of heart and mind that will be ours for the rest of eternity. Let us not wait another second or another minute, and let's start living today in our community of believers around the fellowship table of the Lord. You and I, if we want, can truly live today with a new song and the new language of faith, hope, and love. Let's move forward. Open ourselves to the ministry of the Lord's love feast, loving one another with the grace of God. People are waiting to hear our voices. *When the heart speaks, the hearts will answer. The evidence of our changed heart is that we become heart-changers.*

I am not asking God for more words to preach to others; I am seeking the Lord to receive the kind of language that would engage Him in conversation so I have a true, faithful relationship with Him. I am not asking God for another display of His power; I am crying out for more of the deep assurance of his love that overwhelms me with the reality of his forgiveness, mercy, and compassion towards me. I am not looking for more songs so I can record a new worship album and conduct another successful Christian concert; I am longing for the kind of heavenly sounds that, when I am alone with my Savior, will bring sacred romance to the heart of God. I crave the authentic intimacy that transforms me into His image. I am not asking for a big church, a large crowd, or a huge auditorium; I am asking for the privilege of gathering around those who share these same prayers and desires in their hearts. I will spend all I have over and over again, go anywhere I need to go, sacrifice whatever needs to be lost, pay the price I must pay to find such a place, such a person, such a people, such a community that understands that a life without God is not worth living—that things can only be beautiful and purposeful as long as they stand in proper relationship with Him, who is perfection and beauty itself. I am asking to rehearse this cup of blessing until that day comes when I stand before the marriage supper of the Lamb.

## Proximity is Clarity

In many ways, we have seen how the church's liturgy celebrates the culture of heaven on Earth. One of the ways that our proximity to God is enriched in worship is by the stimulation of the senses. Christianity has always been about the acknowledgment of the goodness of creation. That means for the full experience of embodiment to be engaged in worship, we believe in handling, hearing, tasting, seeing, and smelling things sacred. Remember Thomas when he was confronted by the Lord?

> *"They told him, 'We have seen the Lord!' But he replied, 'I won't believe it unless I see the nail wounds in his hands, put my fingers into them, and place my hand into the wound in his side.' Eight days later the disciples were together again, and this time Thomas was with them. The doors were locked; but suddenly, as before, Jesus was standing among them. 'Peace be with you,' he said. Then he said to Thomas, 'Put your finger here, and look at my hands. Put your hand into the wound in my side. Don't be faithless any longer. Believe!'" (John 20:25-27 NLT)*

The Lord recognizes the limitations of our minds in the absence of physical features. Faith is often viewed as the absence of evidence, when perhaps it should be understood as trusting in the experience of things revealed to our consciousness. The historicity and specificity of

Jesus' death and resurrection are highlighted by the New Testament sign of the bread and wine. Space, time, and matter are evoked in the liturgy, and at the same time challenged by our faith. Jesus was here doing what we are commanded to repeat in remembrance of him. That brings focus and clarity to the continuity of our world and our existence within time. We are part of God's world, the very same world he visited, affirmed, and preserved by His own power. Yet that is not all that our senses allude to in the liturgy of the Eucharist, because as we handle the sacraments, we are challenged to believe He is still here with us in the bread and wine. That means the Lord is operating within creation in new ways that defy our understanding. My personal understanding of this is to say that in the ritual of the Lord's Supper, we are celebrating that creation as we understand it has already been transformed. Why not believe it and act like it in the very ritual the Lord instituted to uplift this truth? By lifting the cup, we are transcending time, for we are uniting with the cross in the past and connecting with the powers of the world to come in the future. In partaking of the elements, we are redefining our experience of matter, for we are tasting the transformation of all things in the glorified body of Christ. We are escaping the limitations of space, because by embracing the sacraments, we are asserting that heaven and Earth are intertwining in the midst of our worship. By the way, I don't think this grace is limited to the celebration of the bread and wine of the kingdom. But I think this experience is probably more accentuated in communion, because the emphasis on the engagement of the senses forces us to rethink the specificities of our dogma. Why bread and wine? Who can officiate the rite? Who is permitted to participate and why? The Lord's Supper takes spirituality out of the clouds of ethereal mysticism and grounds us into common humanity. Where do we commune? With whom and why?

## A Little of My Personal Experience

When I started to teach on this subject, our ministry was heavily attacked. There was an exodus from our church and resentment against us from some of our closest friends. It was senseless; all I did was emphasize the forgiveness of the Lord's table, and now I was being perceived as the enemy of the church. Here I am preaching to love one another as Christ loved us, and everyone I had given my life for in ministry was abandoning me. Many of the ones who left acted as if they had never known me. I am not trying to be dramatic, but this is the truth, and as God is my witness, these people were family to me. Many lived at my house, they traveled with me, I discipled them in the faith, married them, presented their children, etc. Yet without notice, they disappeared. I was forced to understand this phenomenon as an attack on the vision of the Lord's table. Jesus faced the same dilemma in John 6:66 when he started to speak on eating his flesh and drinking his blood. There is something inherently offensive about the sacramental theology of partaking of the true body and blood of our Lord. I am not talking about the endless debates throughout church history about transubstantiation vs. symbol. The disciples who walked away from Jesus' ministry could have cared less about the intricacies of the supernatural bread of the kingdom. The problem was that this was too hard for them; this level of commitment, devotion, and consecration required them to give up too much of themselves. It was like saying to Jesus, "Lord, I love you, but not so much as to eat your bloody sacrifice imitating your death."

Nobody wants that much of themselves invested in relationships with others. That kind of devotion demands an uncomfortable exposure of our true selves. It is perceived by the majority of believers as too rudimentary and archaic. For many, this kind of submission seems too specific and personal for their liking. They would rather generalize their faith away from anything localized in actual people, times, places, and events. We don't mind playing the religion of church, but when you call to make our faith official, we get reluctant. It's like the people who live together for years, but when they finally make it official by getting married, suddenly they want to get a divorce. The problem is not with the person they love, or with being in a relationship with someone, the struggle lies in entering into covenant. To be so exclusive, confined, and restricted that you have to give up something of yourself unto another is too much to ask for somebody that is full of themselves. Only those hungry and passionate for oneness with God will respond to this type of vocation. The people that are desperate and thirsty for true eternal covenant will be the only ones attracted to this level of abandonment.

When I was facing all this opposition, I decided to preach even more on the subject of the Lord's Supper. I started to offer the elements regularly in every service, and interesting things started to happen. I know that what I am about to share is going to sound absolutely nuts, because I myself did not expect or believe the experiences that I started to encounter, yet I am sharing these stories for the purpose of opening your mind to the principle of clearly apprehending different spiritual realities by proximity to the senses. Martin Luther mentions in his writings three benefits of partaking of the sacrament: the building of community, assurance of forgiveness, and renewed life in Christ. We saw not only these three blessings increased greatly in our congregation, but also some strange manifestations in the partaking of the bread and wine. I will only mention a few so you don't believe that I have lost my mind. On a certain season, I called for a whole month of communion services, and on the first Sunday I officiated the ceremony I tasted of my cup of grape juice, and the flavor was to me as the taste of wine. I never mentioned anything to anyone, since I do not have any point of reference for how to interpret this phenomenon. Yet I took it as something personal for me, maybe for the building or encouragement of my faith. The second strange occurrence happened during the same month on the third communion service; this time, the grape juice that was in our symbolic jar on the communion table for illustration seemed to multiply itself. It was supposed to have half a glass in the jar, and we filled two cups all the way to the top with the jar still full. Now, I don't know what these signs mean. And it doesn't matter whether or not you believe this sort of thing can really happen. The reason I am sharing these testimonies is to open your mind to some specific concepts.

Because of these experiences, it was unavoidable that I started to view the moment of the consumption of the cup with more expectation and reverence. I greatly anticipate receiving signs of blessings of all sorts now for those participating in the elements. Second, something else began to change in my perspective because of the second experience I described, the multiplication of the juice. I started to view the vessels that were used in those special moments in a different light. For example, I saved the multiplied juice and wondered: what should I do with it? I now keep that jar and glass on the altar at church as a testament of my appreciation for such experiences. What am I trying to say—that you should idolize the utensils of communion, like the Old Testament tabernacle? No, what I am saying is that communion services make my treatment of Christianity much more grounded in specifics. I want now to celebrate the feast more accurately, discerning better the body in all of its implications. Revere the rite as what it was truly meant to be—a holy moment of divine transaction between heaven and Earth. It matters with whom I celebrate it, and how and where the ceremony is conducted. Everything that occurs in the congregation is seen differently because of the engagement of all my senses in what happens in sacramental worship.

# Conclusion

Coming full circle, we can finish where we started. When I look back now at the movie *The Passion of the Christ*, I know how difficult it is to sit at the same table as the Lord. Just like it was a challenge for the disciples at Passover to recollect all the drama of belonging to the people of Israel, persecuted and oppressed through the centuries and surviving under foreign domination, so it is for us today to sit at a table that, when celebrated properly, becomes subversive and dangerous to the powers of this world. To leave all things behind and trust in the company of a diverse group of people is as terrifying now as it was back then. This leader in whom we are placing all our hopes and dreams is radical and controversial, and doesn't seem interested in following most of our social and cultural conventions. He breaks all the norms, and he doesn't adopt any of the worldly patterns we esteem so high and precious in our fallen nature. To be in his fellowship is by necessity to be misunderstood and criticized, perceived as living in the fringes of strange fanaticism. To recreate the mysterious power of the Lord's Supper today, we must go beyond the idea that it is sufficient to only perform the rite. The remembrance could definitely assist us to get closer to the model of what it means to become Christ's community. But only if it is accompanied with the vision of pursuing the sacramental life—if not, our memorializing will become the deceptive idolization of empty rituals. Only those broken at this table will comprehend the wisdom of God in his judgments. Forgiveness, humility, and love are the most powerful weapons against the powers of darkness that rule our world. We are in the midst of a spiritual battle that can't be fought by natural means. There is no way to comprehend the depths of the work of God in the humanity of Jesus separated from His fellowship table. All His actions and words, even His very sacrifice on the cross without His communal meal, become elusive to the senses and totally distorted to the mind. Do we actually think we really know Jesus? What it really was like to sit in his little flock of followers? Commitment and consecration are never small pills to swallow. But the mission and vocation with which the Lord entrusted his followers was the total expression of His glorious identity in the profound mystery of his complex personhood. This enormous task redefines conflicts, offenses, sufferings, and the overall perception of justice.

> *"Jesus said to them again, 'Peace to you! As the Father has sent Me, I also send you.' After saying this, He breathed on them and said, 'Receive the Holy Spirit. If you forgive the sins of any, they are forgiven them; if you retain the sins of any, they are retained.'"* (John 20:21-23)

The Father sent the Son in the model of a life-giving sacrifice around which his community could be sustained and ultimately glorified. He was sent in the incarnation to take humanity upon himself. He was broken in the restoration of all things on the cross, birthing new creation through his death and resurrection. Then He ascended in his exaltation, seating us with Him in heavenly places to partake of the throne of glory. That is the responsibility and power that rests upon us. Jesus was telling His disciples, "I was sent to share this communion with my body and blood; therefore, do this in remembrance of me." From that position of commissioning, the world looks completely different. We are empowered to redeem, reconcile, and heal our world through forgiveness by the grace of His sacrifice. That glorified body is still breathing upon us today. That miraculous sacrifice continues to release the new creation in the Holy Spirit that is contained and expressed within His community. Everything Jesus did and said is now understood in a new depth, because the example of His divine life has awakened our hearts to become fully alive to the world to which we are sent.

## *Jesus' Perplexing and Controversial Divine Life*

Did you know that on one occasion, Jesus did not go to visit one of the most beloved and appreciated families of his ministry? Knowing that one of his closest friends named Lazarus was deathly ill, he not only didn't go to pray for him to heal him, he let him die on purpose and then did not even attend his funeral. Would you have been offended with Jesus if he did this to you? After you invested in his movement, caring for him with high-quality service and attention in your home, wouldn't it be irritating to see how cruelly he ignored your request for a visit? When he finally showed up late at the grieving home, He said to his close friends:

> *"I am the resurrection and the life. The one who believes in Me,*
> *even if he dies, will live. Everyone who lives and believes in Me*
> *will never die—ever. Do you believe this?" (John 11:26)*

Really? All the people could see at this moment was the fact that, to them, he was showing up too late. It is hard for us to see because of our pain and loss that for God, there are things more important than our immediate validation. Showing us who He really is in all of His splendor and beauty is the priority of His kingdom on Earth, even if it comes by the disappointments and pain of death itself. The sufferings, betrayals, contradictions, and anomalies of life are the best opportunities to move beyond our personal offenses and discover hidden divine beauty in dark places. That he did not care enough to show up in time needs to give way to the fact that something bigger than their loss and bitterness needed to be revealed to leave behind a legacy that would live on beyond their generation. Living alongside the Lord and being one of his followers meant that the drama of life was going to be met head on, in all of its fullness. We will cry, complain, be irritated, get frustrated, and often feel forgotten and forsaken, only to realize how in all those facets of life, there is always something deeper than what our natural minds may perceive. If you reduce Jesus' body to the level of attachment based on preferential treatment, God will allow everything you hold dear to eventually die in your arms to force you to trust him for a real connection that is grounded in the truth of resurrection, and not on superficial emotionalism.

Nowadays it is very difficult for people to accept that Jesus did not fulfill many of the expectations of those who loved and followed him, because he was operating on another plane of reality that is not easily apprehended by our senses—unless we come to his world, learning how to commune with him and dine at his kingdom table. In one instance, Jesus even denied his own relatives, his mother and his brothers, the attention requested from him. Not only did he completely ignore them by not giving them access to his presence, but he publicly scorned them, telling everyone present that the only family he had were those who would hear his word and do the will of his Father in heaven. If you were a member of Jesus' family, would you have expected better treatment? You probably would have liked a bit more consideration. How difficult it is to humanize Jesus, right? To take him out of the clouds and place him in real-life scenarios. How heavy it is to apply his life to our contemporary events! Even if no one comprehended or could appreciate the realization that Jesus' commitment to his community was superior to every human bond on Earth, including those of his own family, he still needed to stand up for that witness. It did not matter if the very ones surrounding him as his disciples did not deserve his full attention or would eventually walk away from him. Where the ideal alliance and loyalty should be placed on this Earth was a worthy enough reason to let everyone know that divine perspectives do not follow worldly ethics and customs. If you are so family-centered that you prefer the affections of the flesh over the reverence for his body, your idolatry will cause Jesus' kingdom agenda to eventually offend you and become a stumbling block for your faith.

Did you know that on one occasion Jesus appeared in the temple of Jerusalem, the most sacred and holy place on the planet, and began a riot? He overturned tables, demolished furniture, broke ornaments, and threw blows with a whip, without any warning. If you were present in the temple that day to worship, would those actions have seemed a bit extreme or exaggerated to you?

I wonder what opinion we would have if we listened to some of Jesus' live messages today. In the midst of his preaching, he stopped to call many leaders of his day vipers, murderers, snakes, hypocrites, bleached sepulchers full of dead men's bones! Reading Jesus' discourses, we see that on more than one occasion he called people names—like Herod, who he deemed a fox. He insinuated that others were like pigs, a perverse generation, fools and children of the devil. Perhaps this is all too harsh, intense, or difficult to accept for our modern paradigms of spirituality. But within Jesus' worldview of integrated reality, he was holding the tension between judgment and mercy, honoring the mediations and transactions necessary to uphold both grace and truth. Everything he confronted on Earth was climatically moving towards the consummation of all things on his cross. He was going to address, absorb, and redefine all the weight of fallen creation. The temple he was symbolically destroying was the old order of things that, in the judgement upon His own body, will be rendered obsolete. The confrontation he was verbally battling was against all the forces of darkness, which manipulated humanity into opposing the change that was about to manifest in his own person. Jesus was generally misunderstood because he was too human to be embraced by the carnal-minded. He took the liberty to do the will of his Father, and gave himself the space to live out his humanity to all its fullness.

In actuality, Jesus was never sinning against anybody but only showing his humanity—the feelings of being touched with the limitations and complications of having a shared life in his earthly existence. He was doing whatever it took to get our attention. He was leading in the way that was required of him to stretch us out of our comfort zone and cause us to transcend our traumatized and crippled identity. Humanly speaking, Jesus always gave his best to God and others, but even after all that energy, for many around him all his efforts were not enough. They wanted even more! They never wanted more of God's example for their lives. They wanted more of their preferences and earthly cravings, based on their superficial opinions of what is correct in their own sight. Jesus did not grant their wishes. He was resolute in not rejecting his own convictions. He refused to be the puppet of the carnal appetites of the self-righteous and the worldly religious system. He was about to shut the whole system down and turn the power back up again, renewing all creation into a new state of consciousness. Jesus preferred to be misinterpreted and perceived as offensive rather than reduced to a mere social effort for the temporary relief of our lifestyle. He chose to be criticized and blasphemed by others before ending up as a sectarian cultural phenomenon. Did you know that practically everything that Jesus did in his time was deemed scandalous and controversial? He had twelve ignorant assistants, women as disciples, a thief as a treasurer, a foul-mouthed leader, and a former terrorist as an apostle. Not to mention the national traitor, Matthew, who was a Jewish tax collector for Rome. All these were part of his ministerial group. He was known as the friend of publicans and sinners, a heavy drinker and glutton. How do you think he earned that stigma? By trying to be very careful about how the people perceived him and the optics of his good public image? Far from it! He was so free from us that he was able to give himself completely to us.

> *"This is why the Father loves Me, because I am laying down My life so I may take it up again. No one takes it from Me, but I lay it down on My own. I have the right to lay it down, and I have the right to take it up again. I have received this command from My Father." (John 10:17-18)*

To reveal the glory of God, Jesus had to unmask the hearts of all men and uncover the hidden intentions of the iniquity buried inside all human rebellion. Such delicate, supernatural, and divine work cannot be achieved by trying to influence people and seeking to sympathize with the masses. For Jesus to reveal the glory of his Father, he had to offend the carnal-minded and awaken the lost appetites of the souls and hearts of man. Most Christians today are still not human enough to understand this deep reality. Only when we properly celebrate the Lord's Supper will we see the glory of the cross and the true humanity of the eternal Jesus, who is still revolutionizing our misconceptions and presuppositions. This table is extremely dangerous for those who love to pretend. The Lord is only interested in hearts and souls that are ready to open up and be loved, until that love overflows in gratitude and forgiveness towards those that reveal the face of Jesus Christ at his table in the meal of the kingdom.

Made in the USA
Monee, IL
18 March 2022

93084187R00121